Carved Gifts
for All Occasions

Carved Gifts
for All Occasions

100 Simple Projects
for the Woodcarver

James E. Seitz, PhD

Linden Publishing

Fresno

Carved Gifts for All Occasions
100 Simple Projects for the Woodcarver

By
James E. Seitz
Cover art by James Goold

© 2006 Linden Publishing

135798642

ISBN: 0-941936-95-3
ISBN 13: 978-0-941936-95-8
Printed in Thailand

Library of Congress Cataloging in Publication Data

Seitz, James E.
    Carved gifts for all occasions : 100 simple projects for the woodcarver / by James E. Seitz.
        p. cm.
    ISBN-13: 978-0-941936-95-8 (pbk. : alk. paper)
    ISBN-10: 0-941936-95-3 (pbk. : alk. paper)
1. Wood-carving. 2. Gifts. 3. Jewelry making. I. Title.
TT199.7.S445 2006
731.4′62—dc22

200617734

Linden Publishing Inc.
2006 S. Mary
Fresno CA
www.lindenpub.com
800-345-4447

Photo 1: The excellence of a gift lies in its appropriateness rather than in its value. —Charles Dudley Warner (1829-1900)

Contents

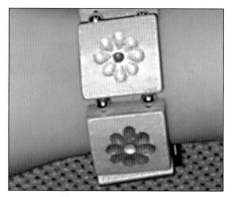

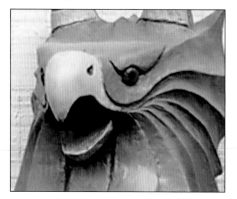

Dedication

This volume is affectionately dedicated to my wife, Arlene, and our daughters and son, Diane, Ellen, Linda, and Karl.

Acknowledgements

Credit for helping to make this work meaningful is hereby given to several individuals. Tom Meyer, friend and fellow woodcarver, deserves an expression of gratitude for allowing me to include in the book a photographic copy of his superbly carved bear. I am equally appreciative of the assistance given by my immediate family and several younger descendants. Heartfelt thanks goes to Linda Winkler, my youngest daughter, for modeling a set of jewelry, to Ellen Gates, my second daughter, for her invaluable help with transcript filing via computer, to Diane Adams, my oldest daughter, for frequently assisting with photography and by modeling, to Diane's granddaughters, Kaila Bivens and Zoe Michalik, for modeling pieces of jewelry, and to Arlene, my dear wife, for helping by taking pictures and for her assistance in other ways.

Introduction

This book is replete with ideas. It contains illustrations of 100 different carved articles suitable for giving as gifts. From the extensive variety shown, an appropriate gift can be identified for virtually anyone on any holiday, celebrated occasion, or personal event. The text answers questions primarily about what to give and the various occasions for giving.

In order to fulfill its purpose, the book devotes only limited coverage to methods of construction. While the text is not a step-by-step instructional manual, many of the articles shown are accompanied with helpful hints for their construction or for designing similar pieces. Descriptions of size often accompany the illustrations. Thus, a woodcarver having no more than elementary experience should be able to proceed effectively. Those already possessing that beginning level of knowledge and skill in woodcarving have no need for instructions on performing the basic procedures of construction.

While a fundamental knowledge of woodcarving is essential, knowing how to use woodworking equipment can be helpful. By and large, the sawing and planing of wood to size is seldom done by hand these days, and purchasing stock prepared for carving can be expensive. Moreover, thin pieces of the kind used in making small carvings might not, except on rare occasions, be available commercially. Having a few pieces of power equipment available will suffice for preparing the stock needed for carving and assembling.

Most of the gifts recommended do not utilize large pieces of wood. That is particularly true for jewelry. Women and girls are inclined to be most interested in small items carved for personal adornment. Bangles, expansible bracelets, necklaces, brooches, earrings, and barrettes are among the variety illustrated and recommended for them. The hat pins, bolo ties,

tie clasps, and name tags suggested for men and boys also require the use of small, relatively thin pieces of wood.

Besides the various items for embellishing personal attire, carved articles are illustrated and described that range in variety from humorous creatures designed to protrude from a shirt pocket to serious items for use while walking for one's health. Attractively designed containers for practical use about the home and decorative items for hanging on a wall add to the variety. The woods used vary, too, from weathered wood in rustic form to those milled and assembled into highly finished articles. Different styles of carving are treated, from naturalistic to abstract, and so are the various carving methods. Chip carving, relief carving, and carving in the round are among them. The details included enable one to fashion subjects suitable for awarding to virtually anyone on any occasion whatever.

The pieces illustrated may be copied with confidence. Every piece shown, except one, has been created by the author. Among his credits are: founding president of a woodcarving club, author of several woodcarving books, and designer/woodcarver whose carvings have won ribbons in juried shows. Carvings previously entered in shows are among those illustrated here.

1. Observe the Basics

Gift-giving is an art. Rather than the haphazard practice many people make it, the presentation of a gift appropriate for the person who will receive it requires conscious effort to solve the mystery involved. Knowledge of the recipient's interests addresses one part of that mystery. Another aspect is providing something that has unique value. It need not be elaborate, but it will be considered special if it has that one-of-a-kind quality. An individually carved gift may very well fill the bill.

The benefits of handmade gifts

Experience indicates that handcrafted articles, especially when made by a close friend or family member, are frequently received more favorably than items manufactured in large quantities. The personal attention and devotion that an acquaintance or relative puts into a gift's making will often elicit expressions of appreciation beyond the ordinary. Both adults and youngsters are known to respond favorably upon receiving handmade gifts. As often as not, the reaction is extraordinarily positive.

The fact that woodcarvings are generally appreciated opens an entire area for gift-giving. Males and females of nearly all ages seem to like a wood's warmth and the qualities of individualized construction. Also, the variety of things possible to carve offers opportunities for carving gifts for just about everyone. A notable exception, as emphasized later, is the youngster who has not yet reached a state of maturity for safely handling certain kinds of gifts.

Occasions for giving

Every year is replete with occasions for giving gifts. Many worthy events develop as family and personal needs arise, others occur on dates traditionally acknowledged for special celebrations, and some evolve for no reason other than to create a bit of humor. Christmas, Hanukkah, Valentine's Day, Mother's Day, Father's Day, and Secretary's Day, having been celebrated over the years on days set aside for the various purposes, continue to be widely acknowledged as times for giving. Occasions such as anniversary dates, birthdays, retirement parties, bachelor parties, marriages, graduations, and new home warmings are among the types of individualized events that do not lend themselves to the nationwide recognition accorded those mentioned above. Even the giving of prank packages or gag gifts has now become a thing to do in special instances. A practical joke party at the office, for example, will likely generate a plethora of unique awards.

Whatever the day, whatever the occasion, and whoever the recipient, an appropriate gift can be carved in wood. The many examples given in the chapters that follow are there for the woodcarver to choose among and copy or view as inspiration for one's own creations. The opportunities for moving ahead are practically without limit. One need no more than an elementary knowledge of woodcarving to proceed effectively.

Copying and creating

The woodcarver who has not been working out his or her designs by sketching should learn to do so (**Photo 2**). That practice will save considerable time and expense in the long run. Sketching on paper is useful in design, but it is only the first step. The figure must be transferred to the wood in preparation for sawing and carving. Novices often use tracing paper to do that. Experienced hands are more likely to learn to construct a figure's outline directly on the wood.

Designing wooden gifts poses no particular problem, because persons who have limited experience in that area can proceed by first copying finished articles. Originality in design can then be developed as one learns from an exemplary base. Ultimately, the accomplished woodcarver will strive for excellence in design

Photo 2: *The woodcarver who has not been working out designs by sketching should learn to do so.*

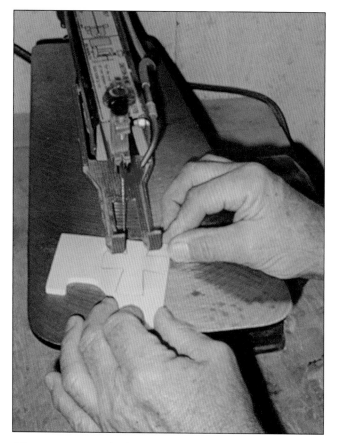

Photo 3: As with this scroll saw, equipment should be used with the guard in place.

to complement his or her carving skill.

If desired, many of the wooden articles represented and discussed in this book may be altered in design. The possibilities are extensive. Minor changes or complete substitutions in style, form, or method of carving are often possible, and many of the floral, animal, and abstract configurations shown can be refashioned to accommodate individual preferences. Gifts in very large numbers would then be available to choose from, if one adds to the designs given the various alterations that might be made.

Material and equipment

A basic requirement in carving is wood that will cut cleanly. This is particularly true when making detailed carvings of jewelry. That with a homogeneous grain is often best for such applications. Basswood is generally suitable, but

a slightly superior wood for small or intricate pieces is tupelo. It has a homogeneous grain, is strong, incises easily, and will firmly hold carved detail without the fuzziness sometimes resulting when carving basswood.

Other woods, such as butternut, cherry, and walnut, will also do if the natural color of their grain is desired. Utilitarian bowls and trays are examples in which the appearance of the wood's grain is usually considered an asset. For some applications, the whiteness of tupelo and basswood may be better if stained or painted. Chip-carved items in those woods are rarely colored.

Individuals who have a basic knowledge of using power tools ordinarily kept in a wood shop are not likely to encounter difficulty in making gifts as recommended. The craftsman who has that knowledge can prepare wood for carving as deemed fitting. That, indeed, will be a distinct advantage, for to make many of the articles displayed hereafter the wood must be thinned or roughed to shape. Tools for sawing, smoothing, and sanding are useful. A circular saw or a band saw, can be an indispensable tool for ripping thin pieces from stock. Thinning and smoothing can then be accomplished by jointing and planing. Devices for power sanding are useful, as well. In any case, power equipment built with a guard should be operated with that device in place and always according to the manufacturer's recommendations **(Photo 3)**.

As to finishing, carved pieces are often given nothing more than a coat of clear, satin sealer. This allows the natural beauty of the wood to show through without a glossy sheen. When attempting to duplicate nature, however, realistic portrayals of animals in woods of homogeneous grain may be enhanced with the use of stain or acrylic paints. To prohibit acrylics from spreading throughout the wood's pores, a thin spray of sealer can be applied before brushing on the colors. Sometimes, too, the acrylics must be allowed to dry completely before applying adjacent colors. A final spray of clear polyurethane will then brighten and protect the finished work.

Construction and safety practices

Construction is relatively simple. While an elementary knowledge of woodworking is generally adequate, an ability to do small-scale detailing with carving tools may be the only special skill required. Besides having a variety of gouges and knives on hand, the woodcarver might also profit by having a small power carver available for occasional use.

As regards safety, power equipment and tools should be used carefully. Hand tools, including carving tools, should be kept sharp and should always be used in a manner that does not endanger the hands or body. Fundamental knowledge in this area is adequate, but persons who have not yet learned how to keep tools sharp and use them safely are advised to first learn those basics. In short, the reader should have acquired elementary knowledge and skill in using tools properly before proceeding to make any of the gifts recommended in this book.

The making of jewelry requires special consideration. This necessitates knowing what findings will be attached and how to configure the carvings to receive them. Each class of jewelry uses different devices, that is, different findings for holding parts together or for fastening the carvings in place. Crafts stores often carry jewelry findings. A large variety may also be viewed and purchased online via computer.

Persons of all ages may be given articles like those shown in this book. The most obvious exceptions are very young children. Although mothers have been observed having a child's earlobes pierced for earrings while the little one was still in diapers, one should not place small items of any kind (whether of wood or any other material) on or near a youngster who habitually puts things into its mouth. The dangers from swallowing and choking on an article must be guarded against. Children of kindergarten age and beyond are ordinarily mature enough to receive and handle a carved gift safely. Nevertheless, parents must analyze each situation and act responsibly in this matter.

Photo 4:   Tupelo wood has the qualities desired for carving and maintaining subtle detail.

2. So You're a Year Older

What can I give this year? That, very likely, is a matter of concern for every conscientious person confronted with an upcoming birthday. The answer could be something with a personal touch.

Gifts for adults and children

Birthdays are commonly acknowledged with gifts. Daughters, sons, sisters, brothers, mothers, fathers, grandparents, grandchildren, and close friends are among those awarded mementos annually in recognition of each one's date of birth. Although often a reason for joking and merriment, advancement in age another year has truly become a celebratory event and a time to acknowledge personal preferences.

Most females like jewelry. Whether young or old, the affinity is evident. One need only turn to the advertisements retailers run repeatedly to get an idea of the extent to which jewelry has become popular among them.

Males, on the other hand, often prefer gifts of a different kind. This is not to say they avoid accessories for wearing apparel. Neither does it mean that males do not wear jewelry similar to that worn by women. While many will wear hat, tie, or lapel adornments of neutral or masculine design, some may also be seen wearing chokers and stud earrings. Many, however, prefer things less feminine, sometimes revealing an inclination for things humorous and grotesque. The point is to know a person's likes and dislikes, which could considerably narrow the options for carving a desirable article for his birthday.

Carve a brooch for that birthday

An item of jewelry that offers almost unlimited opportunities in design is the brooch. Brooches are ornaments made for attaching to garments near the neck (**Photo 4**). They can be fashioned to suit the preferences of women and girls of practically all ages except the very young.

Wooden brooches are generally held in place by bar pins. The attachment of a pin to a brooch's back surface occurs after all carving is done (**Photo 5** and **Photo 6**). The use of glue suitable for fastening metal to wood is essential, and the surface of the metal pin to be placed against the wood should first be abraded with sandpaper to clean it of any burrs and assist in obtaining a secure bond. Additionally, a flat area is needed on the back of the wood to accommodate the mating parts. That seldom presents a problem, because many, though not all, of the backs of brooches are left flat.

As the accompanying examples indicate, naturalistic and stylized interpretations of animal and floral life are appropriate. The figures are carvings about 2 inches across the front and 9/16 of an inch thick. Both are made from single pieces of wood. The dove is tupelo turned yellowish from the transparent finish, and the flower is partially painted basswood. Its center simulates pistils. The texturing there is the result of embossing with the hollow-ground tip of a nail, as is the indented eye of the dove. An application of satin polyurethane leaves a slight sheen on the surface of each carving.

The built-up brooch shown in **Photo 7** is an unusual stylization. While representing a four-leaf clover, it derives much of its uniqueness from the lamination of two species of wood. The lighter wood is tupelo. The other is papaw. The latter, shown cut for carving and overlaying in **Photo 8,** next page, is part of the naturally greenish heartwood of the tree.

To construct the clover, pieces are planed to 1/4 inch thickness and sawed to outline in preparation for carving. The papaw overlays are then carved for gluing to the tupelo base, the size of which would fit neatly into a 2 inch

Photo 5:   *Some brooches can be enhanced by the judicious application of acrylic paint.*

Photo 6:   *A strong adhesive and a close fit are important when attaching bar pins.*

Photo 7:   *This stylized four-leaf clover shows the artistic liberty acceptable in design.*

Photo 8:   *Much of the carving of the tupelo and papaw woods precedes their assembly.*

Photo 9:   *A dowel attached to the back of each small piece assists in holding while carving.*

square. Being small, the overlays can be more easily held for carving if each piece is drilled 1/8 inch deep into the back to accommodate the tip of a dowel rod of equal diameter (**Photo 9**). Each overlay should be cut so that the grain will seem to radiate outward from the flower's center in the assembly. Once carved and sanded, the mating surfaces may be covered with wood glue and clamped in place until set.

Touch-up carving, a final sanding, and attaching the bar pin are next in order before applying the finish. To preserve and enhance the grain and colors, a clear sealer is applied. This may be done by spraying on a uniform coat while the brooch sets within a cardboard carton. That arrangement helps contain the excess spray and thereby effectively avoids collateral damage.

Give a necklace of special design

Necklaces of cord or chain designed for supporting ornaments may contain either a single carved pendant or groups of beads and spacers among several carvings. Ordinarily, a necklace containing a single carving is the easier to make.

The carving of a pendant virtually duplicates the procedure previously explained for making brooches. This holds true throughout most stages of construction. After working out a design, the wood is selected and prepared, the design transferred to it, the piece sawed to shape, and the carving begun (**Photo 10**). The similarities are such that some carvings can be made into either a brooch or a pendant.

The woodcarver should be aware of possible differences, however. Articles prepared for use as pendants will be somewhat superior if carved on both sides, especially when made for a youngster. This might not be a matter of utmost importance, but it is worth considering. The advantage of having a pendant carved both front and back is that the wearer need not be as careful about which side faces forward when closing the catch on the necklace's loop. Twisted loops do sometimes result in a pendant's reversal.

Photo 10:   A carved figure can sometimes be made into either a pendant or a brooch.

To be used as a necklace, a small eyelet (sometimes called a "burning pin") is glued into a hole drilled in the carving's upper edge at its center of balance. A chain or cord is then threaded through the eye to form the necklace. A split ring may also be inserted into the eyelet to permit easier insertion of the loop's clasp and allow the pendant to move more freely (**Photo 11**).

The importance of knowing a recipient's interests becomes clearly evident if the carving has a religious orientation. The giving of a wooden cross, such as illustrated in **Photo 12,** provides an example of a pendant necessitating this special attention. Unlike the elephant pendant, the piece is profoundly symbolic (**Photo 13**). It represents only one of many possible designs for both laminated wood and religious symbolism.

A more elaborate ornament may be seen in the kind of necklace assembled using carved elements interspersed among beads and hollow

Photo 11:   Young girls are most likely to accept pendants of animals as prized possessions.

Photo 12:   This laminated cross is an excellent gift for a person of a particular orientation.

Photo 13:   The carving of this pendant is limited mainly to the front of the top piece.

Photo 14: A composite of carvings and spacers is a more elaborate style of ornamentation.

Photo 15: This necklace with its balanced carvings is effectively done in compatible colors.

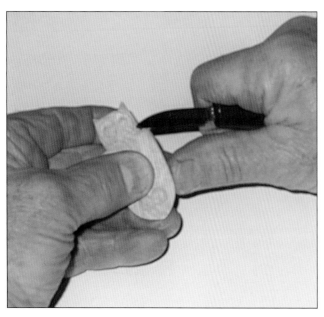

Photo 16: The carving of the owls can be readily accomplished while holding them in the hand.

wooden spacers. Refer to **Photo 14**. The three floral-like figures are carvings made from wood native to Jamaica, while the other items have been purchased at a variety store. All have holes lengthwise, some having been enlarged by drilling to receive the cord.

The necklace's parts are arranged for assembling. All items to be threaded onto the cord will be left movable and balanced in the finished assembly. As to size, the two small pieces are cut from wood 1-1/4 inches across and 3/8 inch thick. The large piece is 1-5/8 inches across and 3/8 inch thick. All of the carved pieces are shaped on both sides.

A built-up variety of necklace that a young girl would probably be most happy to receive and wear features a display of animals. Carved owls, **Photo 15**, and spacers of compatible design are suggested. All should be arranged symmetrically for a balanced effect. Made as recommended, the owls are cut from butternut and held by hand when carving (**Photo 16**). The small ones are 3/4 of an inch wide by 1-3/8 inches long, and the large one is 1 inch wide by 2-1/2 inches long. Their thicknesses are 3/8 inch and 1/2 inch, respectively.

Make her day with earrings

As with many necklaces and brooches, wooden ornaments for the ears may be either carved from single pieces or shaped and assembled using multiple pieces. The simplest are the small ones referred to as "stud" earrings.

A finished stud seems to be little more than a large dot in a person's earlobe (**Photo 17**). For best results, it should be made from a colorful hardwood. Cherry wood does nicely and can be made into a sphere 1/4 of an inch in diameter or less. Due to the small size, its shaping could be tedious, although that possibility can be overcome by carving each piece while it remains attached to a rod-like piece of the wood.

Most of the carving, the sanding, and even the attachment of findings with glue can occur before removing the carvings from the supporting wood. A nail file is useful for sanding. When completely finished, a coat of satin polyurethane may be brushed on the wood to enhance it.

Several types of findings are made for attaching earrings. These include a variety of clasps made for use on unpierced earlobes, the straight ear pins and clutches used to hold earrings close to the ear where pierced, such as for studs, and the fish-hook type for dangling an ornament from a pierced lobe. It is important to know which to use when carving a gift.

Fish-hook ear wires are easily identified by their shape. One is shown attached to the back of a built-up earring in **Photo 18**, next page. Notice the three small, incised marks carved onto the back of the piece. That is the author's way of identifying his workmanship with an out-of-the-way "signature" on things he makes.

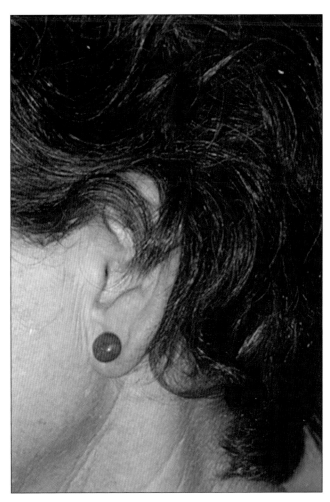

Photo 17:   Stud earrings, this one of cherry wood, are adornments for pierced ears.

Photo 18:   Fish-hook wires on earrings provide a form of attachment preferred by some.

Photo 19:   This pair derives much effectiveness from its nonrepresentational symmetry.

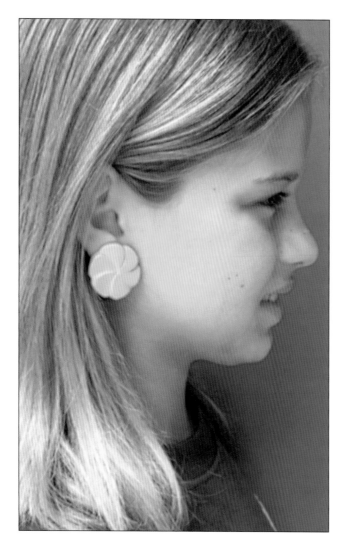

Photo 20:   What young girl wouldn't enjoy receiving earrings on her birthday?

Craftsmen are advised to do something similar with their work, assuming they take pride in what they make.

A front view of the pair of built-up earrings is also presented here (**Photo 19**). They are made of carved laminations of cherry wood, tupelo, and papaw. Each assembly is about 1-1/8 inches wide, 1-1/2 inches long, and 3/4 of an inch thick overall. They are attractive abstractions. Much of their attractiveness is due to the colors, the woods' grain, and the nonrepresentational form. Another factor is the precision with which each curved piece fits against adjacent surfaces.

Earrings in representational style, which some people prefer to any form of nonrepresentational art, portray things with which many humans can readily associate. Whether made totally naturalistic or given a stylized interpretation, a portrayal of some kind of animal or flower will seldom leave any doubt about what it represents. Only an extreme level of abstraction might negate such understanding. That shown being worn in **Photo 20** is a floral stylization.

Pairs of representational carvings are illustrated in **Photo 21** in the form of rabbits and flowers. The wood is basswood, although the centers of the flowers are made of cherry wood for a somewhat more realistic effect. Some realism in

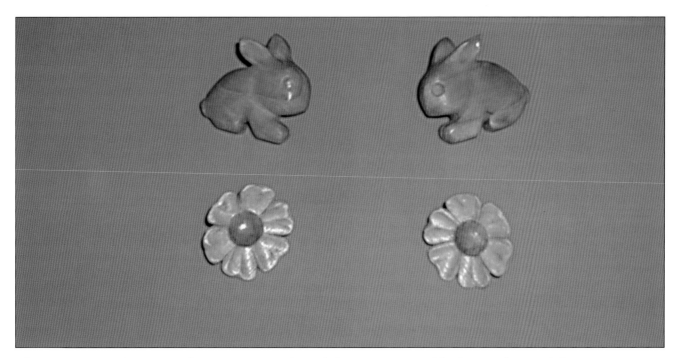

Photo 21:   Carved earrings featuring animals and flowers are suitable for youths or adults.

the rabbits is obtained by the depressions for eyes. That feature is obtained via the use of a nail, **Photo 22**, after having ground the tip to a cupped shape with a Dremel tool.

Both sets have straight pins attached for insertion in pierced ears. Each could be worn by a small person, as the rabbits are only 1-3/16 inches wide, 1-1/16 inches high, and 5/16 inch thick, and the flowers are 7/8 of an inch across the front and 5/16 inch thick. They would make excellent birthday gifts for some adults as well as youngsters.

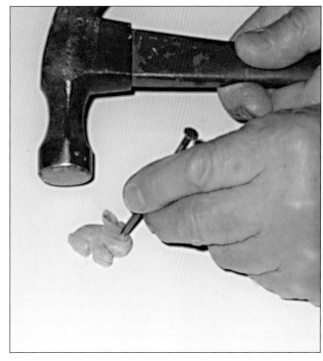

Photo 22:   The rabbit's eyes are embossed using a nail with the tip ground cup-like.

Photo 23:   This view shows the fine painting needed to represent a wood duck naturally.

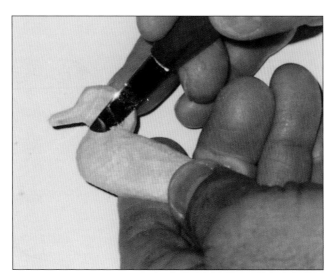

Photo 24:   The detailing of a figure for a hat pin need only be done on one side.

Pins for a man's big day

Just as the previous topics centered on the interests of women and girls, the creation of birthday gifts for men and boys must properly take into account their interests. Hat and lapel pins can be made to reflect various preferences. Here again, knowing a recipient's specific interests is helpful when settling on a design. Animals and outside activities are generally acceptable subjects. Those interested in hunting small game might like a carving of a pheasant or duck, while a big game hunter might prefer a representation of a larger species. On the other hand, those who prefer indoor activities, such as playing a musical instrument, could be most pleased to receive a carving of, say, a piano or drums. Undoubtedly, the possible designs for pins go well beyond these few suggestions.

The relatively small size of a pin made for display on one's hat or coat lapel makes its completion rather quick and easy. Moreover, it may require carving on the face side only. The

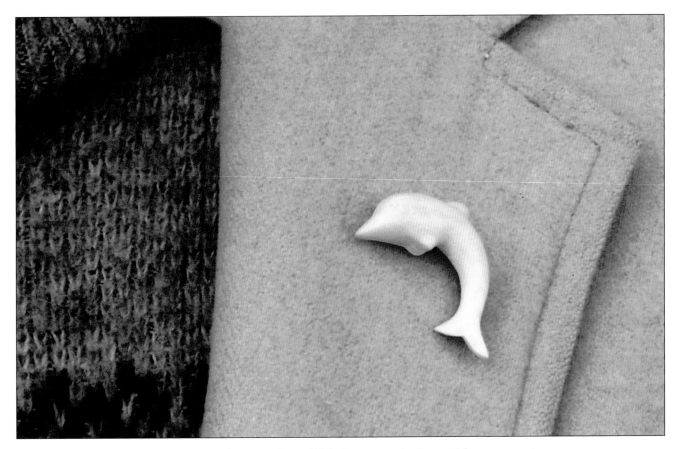

Photo 25: A small dolphin carved in tupelo will likely generate favorable comments.

shaping is then done to a proportionate half depth, leaving the back flat for gluing the pin in place (**Photo 24**).

The colorful wood duck shown pinned to a hat in **Photo 23** requires painting for most effective results. The precision and minuteness involved may be evident in the fact that the figure is cut from a piece of basswood no less than 3/8 inch thick by 1-1/4 inches across the grain and 2-1/4 inches with the grain. As a well-illustrated book of birds shows, the coloring of a wood duck necessitates using a variety of colors and fine detailing for a realistic duplication. Acrylic paint is recommended. The final step, as with all pins (painted or unpainted), is to apply a coat of clear sealer.

The carving of a dolphin, **Photo 25**, offers other considerations. It should be left unpainted, especially if made of a white wood such as tupelo, and its tail should be raised slightly for a realistic effect. Thus, the carving's back should

Photo 26:   A comically styled whale can be a top-notch gift for a fun-loving youngster.

Photo 27:   A voice box wedged in place makes the assembly truly "a whale with a tale."

be left flat throughout except for the tail area where it will be carved completely. It is important to leave an area large enough to receive and hide the lapel pin.

A whale with a tale

A carving certain to make a hit is a comically styled talking whale (**Photo 26**). Give one as a gift to a boy or girl and that youngster will create merriment among friends and visitors for years to come. A voice box with an appealing message will make the piece most effective.

A voice box secured out of view in the whale's bottom, **Photo 27**, with its on-and-off switch easily reached while holding the creation upright, can produce a joyful surprise. A box purchased from a toy store that repeatedly gives a knocking sound and shouts "Let me out of here" when activated is a known winner. Having a box on hand when making the whale helps assure the cavity will be made large enough to hold it. One smaller than the opening presents no insurmountable problem, for a loose fit can be overcome by stuffing plastic packing material about the box's edges. Thus, a cubical box of 3 inches on each side presents no difficulty in an opening 4 inches square and deep or larger.

A loose fit may also simplify replacing the box with another when desired or necessary, perhaps even with a larger one. This suggestion holds true if the whale, itself, is of adequate size. The whale pictured is 6-1/4 inches high, 5-1/2 inches wide, and 12-1/2 inches long. The cavity for the voice box is 3-1/2 inches by 5 inches with a depth of 3-3/4 inches.

The species of wood used matters little, for the whale is painted allover. Spruce or pine lumber used in building framing will do. The whale's construction requires sawing a cavity into the interior piece before gluing the laminations together. Additionally, it requires an ability to shape the external surfaces after the laminations are set. Giving the whale a humorous appearance also requires a bit of skill in carving.

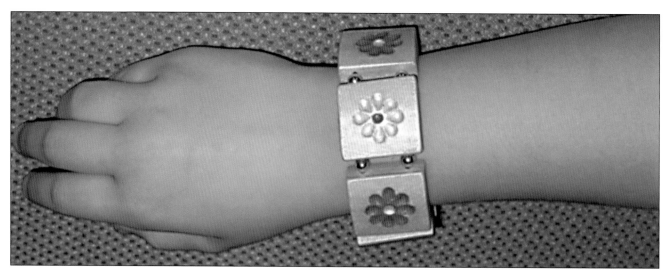

Photo 28:   Expansible bracelets have the wooden sections held in place by elastic cord.

3. Be My Valentine

Seldom is anything more important than being on target with a gift for a loved one on Valentine's Day. Something personally carved that may be displayed with pride can have a lasting and positive effect on one's relationship with a very special friend or sweetheart. Family members often benefit from the celebration, as well. A necklace, earrings, and a brooch done in a single motif for mother, a bolo for father, a bracelet for daughter, and a comical caricature that seems to peep from a shirt pocket for a son are among the variety of possibilities. Identify the person, and a carving as illustrated in this chapter could be just the thing needed for awarding this day.

Valentine's Day is centuries old, but the reason for its origin remains uncertain. Some link the event to the name "Saint Valentine" that was given to one or two legendary Christian martyrs. Some say it has been celebrated traditionally on February 14 in extension of an ancient Roman festival. Others contend the practice stems from an old English belief that birds choose their mates on the particular date

noted, and still others believe the celebration stems from all of those past occurrences and ideas plus the notion that spring is a time for lovers. In any case, the holiday continues to be celebrated worldwide.

Today, the dominant motif appearing in the cards, sweets, and many boxed items marketed for giving on Valentine's Day is the heart. That this symbol has become synonymous with affection and love is evident. Although not every gift to a lover must feature a heart, its presence in the design simply reinforces the underlying thought. There are probably no better instances beyond those occurring on that special day in February for giving such an appropriately decorated gift.

Bracelets from the heart
Ornaments made for wearing around the wrist are a popular part of a woman's and girl's attire. Those fashioned from wood in the form of solid rings are called "bangles," an example of which may be seen in **Photo 29**. Another

Photo 29:   A leaf-and-flower motif is carved repeatedly around the perimeter of this bangle.

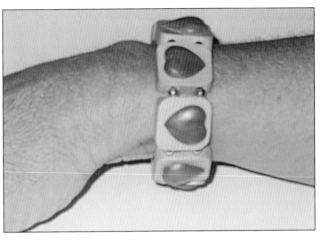

Photo 30:   Laminated woods can be fashioned into a gift appropriate for Valentine's Day.

type, as shown in **Photo 28**, contains a series of block-like shapes held together with flexible cord to provide an expansible quality. The decorative features are open to many possible styles and motifs.

The bangle is cherry wood, 7/8 inch high by 3 inches in outside diameter with a 5/16 inch material thickness. The design is carved in relief and repeated four times around the perimeter. The background is stippled for effective contrast. Being firm and inflexible, the piece can be worn by one who can fold the hand enough to slip the piece into place and wear the piece comfortably. When possible, the making of a bangle should be based on measurements taken around a hand and wrist of the intended recipient.

In keeping with the spirit of the day, an expansible bracelet of repetitive design is shown being worn in **Photo 30**. It, like the bangle, is sized for wearing on a wrist of a particular size. The inside diameter of this piece when not expanded is about 2-1/8 inches.

The bracelet's construction begins by shaping a block of wood so that the inside surfaces will be curved while the outside surfaces will be flat **(Photo 31)**. Doing that provides for a comfortable fit on the wrist and also produces the flat areas needed for gluing the hearts in place. Each heart is roughly carved from cherry wood 1/8 inch thick by 5/8 inch wide and 3/4

Photo 31:   The circle for sawing inside the ring of blocks is sized to the recipient's wrist.

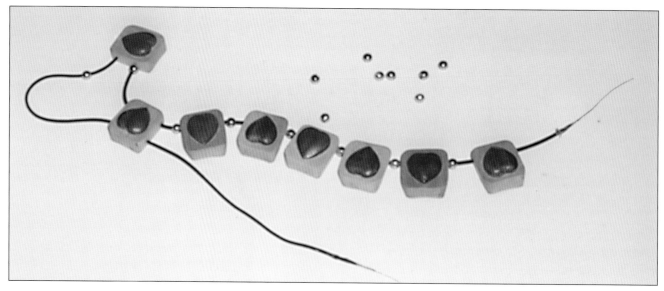

Photo 32:   The blocks are drilled and threaded alternately with beads onto the elastic cord.

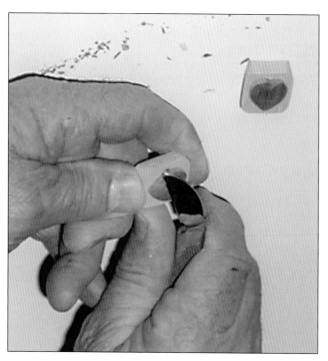

Photo 33:   Hearts of cherry wood are sawed out, glued to the flat surfaces, and then carved.

inch long before being glued to a basswood piece 5/16 inch thick by 7/8 inch square. As indicated in **Photo 33**, the shaping of the hearts proceeds to the final stage of carving and sanding when they are permanently glued in place.

In preparation for assembling, all carved blocks are drilled through in two places to receive the elastic cord that pulls the pieces together after slipping the assembly onto the wrist. Manufactured beads separate the blocks and help cover the two strands of cord. The beads are plastic covered in gold **(Photo 32)**. Be aware that one of the blocks must be drilled slightly different from the others in order to accommodate the beginning and ending points of the elastic cord. It must provide for taking up all slack, gluing the ends fast, and eventually cutting away the excess lengths. A strong glue will hold the cut ends of cord from slipping. The cord must move freely within all blocks except this one which anchors the ends.

Honor her with coordinated jewelry

Jewelry intended for use in sets will satisfy principles of unity and coordination if given a common motif throughout. When worn together on a garment, not only do they seem to go together, they do go together. There is no

Photo 34:   A heart pendant with matching earrings is a beautiful gift for a dear one.

Photo 35:   Sealing the brooch and other parts of the set done in aromatic cedar blocks the aroma.

clashing of designs as might occur with uncoordinated pieces. Imagine, by way of contrast, a pendant shaped like a bear in its natural form being worn next to a brooch carved in some geometric form. The two are simply incompatible. The principle involved is fundamental when designing a set.

What constitutes a set? By definition, any combination of two or more items of jewelry of similar design qualify, but the wearing of no more than three different items at a time is recommended to avoid the appearance of excessiveness. The selection may be taken from among a necklace, a pair of earrings, a brooch, and a bracelet of compatible design.

A necklace, earrings, and brooch in heart motif make an excellent combination for giving on Valentine's Day. See **Photo 34** and **Photo 35**. All pieces are carved front and back. They are made from aromatic cedar of 7/16 inch thickness such that the white streaks common to the wood are not present to detract from the effect of the colorful hearts. The pendant is 2 inches wide, each earring 1 inch wide, and the brooch 2-1/4 inches across.

Size and the wood's density are important. The craftsman should design the several items according to whether the individual who will wear them is a small child or a large person.

Photo 36: Colorful combinations of jewelry are favored by many.

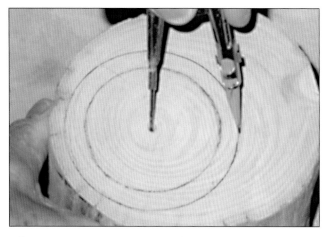

Photo 37: Sawing a bangle's diameters along the wood's rings is recommended practice.

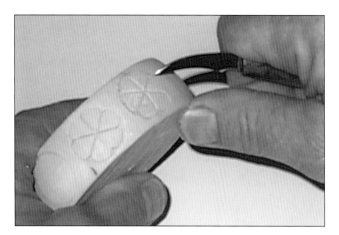

Photo 38: A soft wood cut for a bangle is best carved before hollowing the inside.

Maintaining the relative size of coordinated parts is important, too, and none should be made so large as to be heavy. Weight is particularly critical in the design of earrings.

Another set of jewelry, this one comprised of a pair of earrings, a brooch, and a bangle, is the subject of **Photo 36**. The coordination of pieces is unmistakable in that the wood used throughout is basswood, the design's shape is consistently repeated, and the colors are the same on all pieces. Unlike those in the previous example, the brooch and earrings are left flat on the backside.

Anyone constructing a set of this variety should observe that the bangle's strength is greatest if sawn from a section with the concentric shape closely coincident with the annual rings of the piece from which it is cut **(Photo 37)**. When sawed in that manner, the bangle's design will be laid out and carved on the wood's side grain – a practice far superior to shaping end grain **(Photo 38)**.

Painting, too, has its special precautions. Basswood, being porous and absorbent, will allow acrylic colors to "bleed" into adjacent areas unless the surface is first sealed. A thin coat of polyurethane spray will ordinarily suffice. A final coat of sealer applied after all paints have dried will protect the finished work.

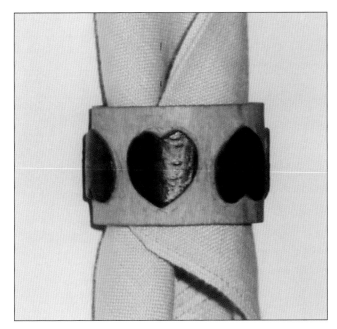

Photo 39:   The bark left on this cherry-wood napkin holder captures the Valentine's Day spirit.

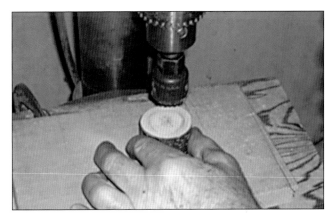

Photo 40:   A hole saw is very useful for removing the center when making napkin rings.

Photo 41:   A paper layout helps space the decorations properly in preparation for carving.

Put some heart into tableware

Does your family include a young married man or woman who is setting up housekeeping? A set of napkin rings just might be the ideal gift for such a person. Make one with a heart design, and you will capture the spirit of the day. Even a rustic one with part of the bark remaining in place may create the interest desired (**Photo 39**).

To make a set of these unique, bark-covered items, begin with a straight branch or sapling about 1-3/4 inches in diameter. It must not be split, but it must have a tight bark that will not peel off when cut into lengths of 1-1/4 inches. A central section 1-3/16 inches in diameter can be readily removed by using a hole saw (**Photo 40**). The design may then be transferred to the outside surface in preparation for removing the bark from all areas except within the outline of the heart shapes (**Photo 41**).

For those who prefer a chip-carved design, the set shown in **Photo 42** affords an alternative. The rings are made from sections of a papaw sapling.

Photo 42:   For a change in style, a chip-carved set could be the kind of useful gift preferred.

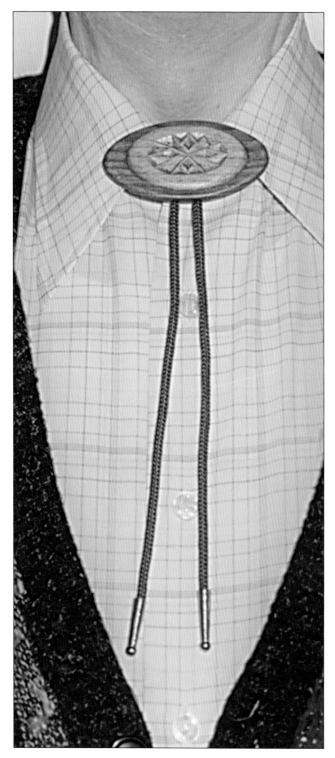

Photo 43: The wearing of a bolo tie in place of a necktie is often a welcome experience.

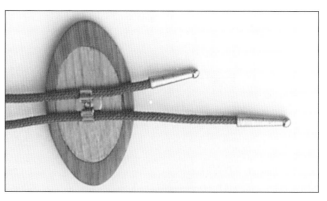

Photo 44: Bolo slides and ferrules are sometimes available where jewelry findings are sold.

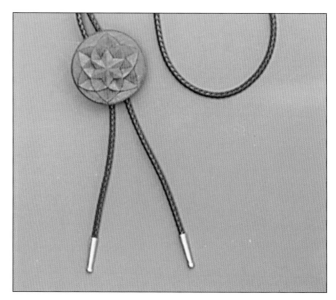

Photo 45: Developing the design is one of the personal benefits of making a carved gift.

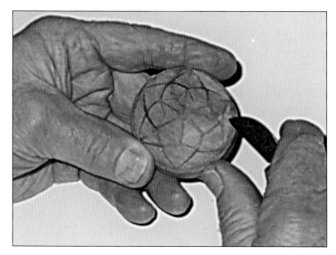

Photo 46: Precision in chip carving depends on having an accurately laid out pattern.

Bolo ties for show and comfort

The bolo tie is a convenient alternative to the traditional necktie. Once assembled, only a simple adjustment is needed with each wearing. The cord is easily slipped under the collar, and the decorative attachment may be firmly snugged or loosely positioned. A chip-carved piece is shown in **Photo 43**. The slide pin on its back, **Photo 44**, provides conveniently for adjusting the tie to the position desired. Although not all men wear bolo ties, there are those who openly extol the virtues of wearing one after years of having tied neckties in place.

The oval piece is made of walnut and butternut woods, with overall dimensions being 1-3/4 inches wide, 3 inches long, and 5/16 inch thick at its center. Accessories for ornaments such as this are sometimes available from suppliers of woodcarving materials. Retailers of jewelry findings even more frequently sell the metal slides, decorative ferrules, and pliable tie cords.

The wooden ornaments in bolo ties are frequently circular in shape. **Photo 45** shows one such carved in pernambuco. The slightly spherical face of the piece is carved in a unique pattern by hand **(Photo 46)**. Its dimensions are 7/16 inch by 2 inches diameter.

As with the 1-3/4 inch diameter bolo pictured in **Photo 47**, circular pieces, especially those designed with a curvature, are preferably first turned and sanded smooth on a lathe **(Photo 48)**. The laminating of pieces precedes the turning, and all carving precedes the sealing and assembling operations. Only in rare instances are chip-carved designs painted or stained before sealing.

Photo 47: A simple but effective design adorns this lamination of tupelo on cherry wood.

Photo 48: A wood turning lathe is helpful when making ornaments with a curved face.

Photo 49:   A wooden frog peering from a shirt pocket may be truly a humorous pocket pal.

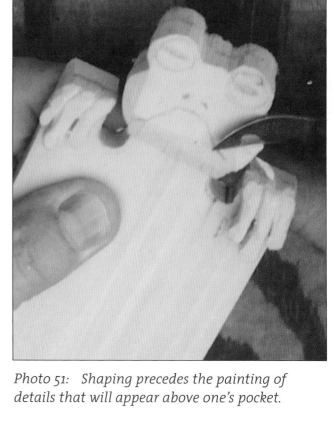

Photo 51:   Shaping precedes the painting of details that will appear above one's pocket.

Photo 50:   The basswood is built-up for purposes of depth at the frog's toes and face.

Pocket pal humor

Want to give something to a youngster who enjoys generating a little mirth among friends? Give a Pocket Pal. Designed to appear to leer or peep over the top edge of a shirt pocket, a small caricature could produce the surprise intended when a sweater or coat is pulled back quickly to reveal the creation.

The carved frog pictured in **Photo 49** is such a creation. Its toes seem to grasp the pocket's edge, while it pokes a bug-eyed head into view. Applications of green, black, and white acrylics in the visible portions give the figure its recognizable features.

The frog's construction begins with a piece of basswood 3-1/8 inches wide, 6 inches long, and 7/16 inch thick. Small pieces are then attached to enlarge the facial area and toes, leaving a gap behind the toes as may be seen in **Photo 50**. Next to occur is the carving of features that will show above the pocket, as well as the rounding

*Photo 52:   This "Hi There Guy" may be a
preferred form of pocket pal.*

of the edge of the board on the front side **(Photo
51)**. After painting and sealing, the frog is ready
for a spot in a pocket.

Do you prefer a different figure? Maybe a
caricature of a somewhat bewildered human
will do. Consider the reproduction in **Photo 52**. If
you're still not satisfied, design a figure to your
liking. The possibilities are limitless.

4. Make that Anniversary Commemorative

Photo 53:   Walking sticks, including naturally twisted ones, are often capped with special carvings.

One of the most thoughtful gifts for a person is an article that will, potentially at least, benefit his or her health. The walking stick is such a piece. It is an easily made device in wood which seems to say "Get up and move. It's your health." Whether given to a spouse in recognition of another year together or to married sons or daughters and their partners on each one's anniversary, the presentation of a neatly adorned piece can be expected to evoke expressions of gratitude. Indeed, the thought behind the giving may be considered as significant as the gift itself.

Here's to your health

The walking stick is truly an instrument for one's well-being. Regardless of style, or whether fashioned from milled lumber or a bark-covered sapling, a straight staff is the kind of companion hikers often carry. In fact, some persons who walk constantly for their health proclaim that they would not feel completely dressed without a good stick in hand. Even more forceful reasoning could be given by partially lame persons who need the assistance of the shorter variety when walking.

Walking sticks are of two basic types: canes and staffs. Canes are comparatively short pieces made to be leaned on for support. Their top ends are finished in a crook or other shape suitable for holding onto at about mid-thigh height. Staffs, by way of contrast, are relatively straight pieces, the lengths of which are more or less equal to shoulder height. They are particularly helpful when walking up hills or when pushing brush aside while walking in wooded areas. They may also provide peace of mind for those concerned about protection and personal safety when walking alone or in isolated places. Both types of aids may be made decorative as well as useful.

Photo 53 shows a walking stick with a ball-in-cage carving attached by mortise and tenon to the upper end of a twisted staff. The carved piece is butternut (1-3/4 inches in diameter by 8 inches long), and the staff is a sassafras sapling with its bark intact. The twist on the sapling is natural due to a honey suckle vine having wrapped about and constricted the small tree during its growth. The twist is counter-clockwise, which is always the direction of entwinement by those vines in the United States.

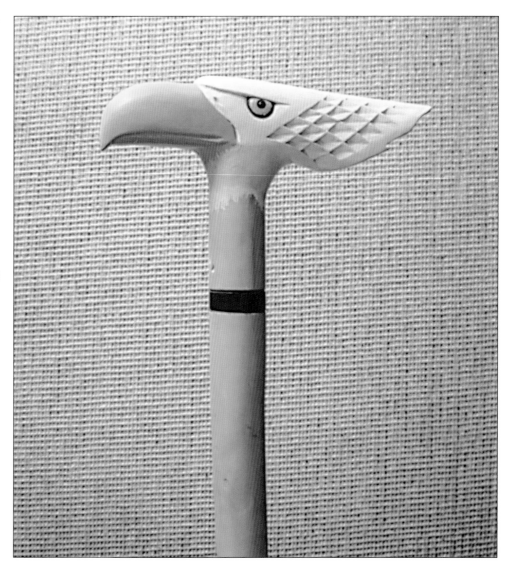

Photo 54:   A carved cane can be decorative as well as serve a useful purpose comfortably.

Although the carving of this spiral configuration may be somewhat advanced for some, woodcarvers at all levels of experience are urged to strive for its mastery. Imagine walking in a busy park with such a piece and the comments of others about it. The pride generated may very well be a reason for always carrying a carved stick on those walks.

Carved canes can also be made decorative without diminishing their useful purpose. The upper part of one is shown in **Photo 54**. The grip, an eagle's head, is a stylized piece carved in the round with chip carving added for a special effect. It is attached to a debarked sapling by the customary use of a mortise and tenon joint. An automotive body filler provides transition from

Photo 55:   This stick, a branch from a pear tree, has small, floral figures incised at each knot.

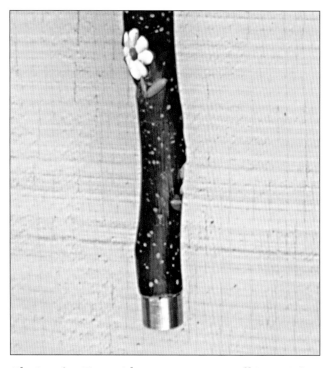

Photo 56:   To avoid excess wear, a walking stick must be protected at its lower tip.

Photo 57:   A round mortise-and-tenon joint is effective for capping a staff.

the stick to the carved piece. The filler has sufficient strength and can be easily carved. Acrylic paints add a bit of realism.

An easily constructed variety of walking stick has small decorations incised along a shaft where branches have emerged and grown. One such is shown close-up in **Photo 55** and **Photo 56**. The stick is a pear branch with flowers carved using a power-driven burr. Its length is 4 feet 8 inches, which makes this type of stick suitable for carrying by individuals of different heights. A common way to cap such staffs may be seen in **Photo 57**.

When designing walking sticks for the use intended, some way of protecting the tip against wear must be considered. A ring of copper tubing of correct diameter fastened to the bottom end of the staff is one solution. Avoiding excessive wear where a stick abrades against the ground may also be achieved by inserting an oval-headed screw driven lengthwise into the tip so that only the head projects.

Although reasons for carrying walking sticks

vary, canes are usually carried out of necessity due to ambulatory difficulty. To be most useful, a cane must be sized for ease in gripping the upper end, and the length must be determined precisely according to the user's requirements. In other words, the length must be such that an individual's grasping hand and stiffened arm will take pressure off the afflicted leg or joint.

The tip of a cane must also be treated specially. Because of the force applied, a cane tends to slip or skid on smooth surfaces. A rubber tip may help solve the problem. Rubber tips in various diameters are available commercially.

Hearts and flowers applications

Anyone designing a walking stick for presentation as an anniversary gift will likely have a particular person in mind. That knowledge can be important for two reasons. First, the length of the stick and placement of the decoration have to be known in order to be certain the piece will function appropriately in the person's hands, and, secondly, the decision about whether the decoration will have a masculine, feminine, or neutral orientation must be decided at the outset. The distinction might not always be clear-cut, but an attempt should be made to determine if the design is likely to be favored more by women than men, or vice versa. For example, which of the sexes do you think would prefer, say, a floral decoration over a carving of a reptile?

A walking stick's length and placement of a decoration are, as one might surmise, properly based on the user's height. Refer to **Photo 58** for purposes of illustration. This staff is suitable for a woman who will grip the piece when walking at a point between the upper end of the yardstick and the stick's circle. That is why the carved hearts are positioned there. They are decorative, but they also serve the important purpose of assisting when walking. As any experienced walker knows, there must be some configuration, or some roughness, present for gripping comfortably. The hand has a tendency to slip downward when walking with a staff that is too smooth. A loop of leather attached at

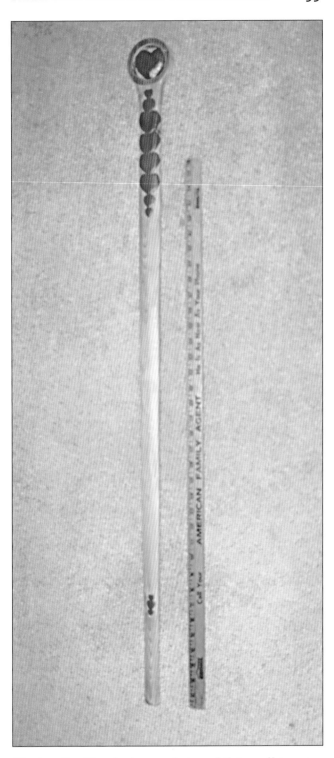

Photo 58:   The design and size of this walking stick make it worthy of giving to one's wife.

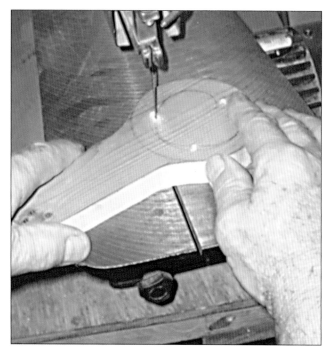

Photo 59:   Scroll sawing to remove wood from internal areas simplifies the carving process.

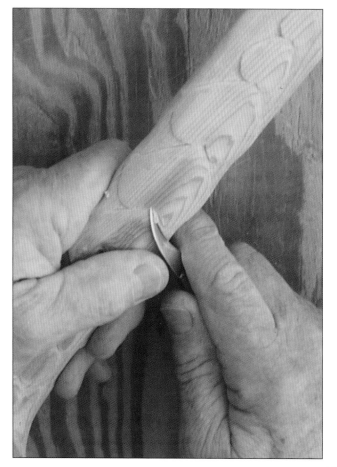

Photo 60:   Even low-relief carvings are useful when placed at a spot gripped when walking.

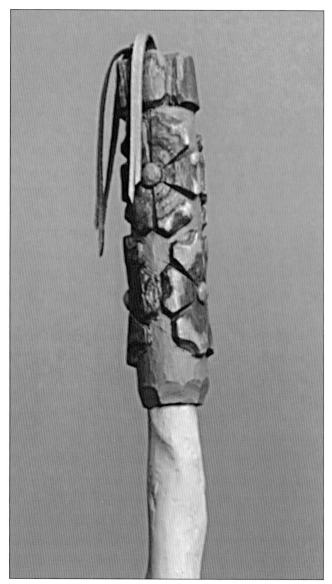

Photo 61:   An alternate design for topping a woman's gift-stick is a floral design in relief.

the proper height will also suffice for gripping.

The most comfortable spot for gripping an erect walking stick is at elbow height. In that way, the user's forearm extends forward and parallel to the ground when standing. The height for a man, in general, would be about 4 or 5 inches more than that used in making the one photographed beside the yardstick.

As may be apparent in the accompanying photographs, the walking stick was sawed from a 3/4 inch pine board (**Photo 59** and **Photo 60**). Its circular head was drilled for inserting a scroll saw blade and cutting away the excess wood about the large heart. This was followed by rounding the shaft by hand planing, laying out the heart design along the shaft, carving the figures in low relief, and brushing on an acrylic paint of suitable color before sealing. The amount of sanding involved was practically nil.

An alternative for a woman's walking stick is a floral design of some kind. A terminal piece in sumac, shown carved in relief in **Photo 61**, provides an example. Paint covers the background of the carving, but the flower heads retain the natural beauty of the wood's grain. In general, the diameter of the piece to be selected for carving should be equal to or slightly greater than the diameter of the stick it decorates.

Bark carving methodology

A unique method of decorating walking sticks is a form of low relief called "bark carving." As the name implies, sections of the bark of a staff are removed to create a pattern. **Photo 62** shows an example. Evident are sections of bark removed to reveal the inner wood and sections left standing. Acrylic paint enhances the pattern.

Bark carving must be done on saplings of easily held thickness that have tight, comparatively smooth bark. Poplar and similar young saplings are good for this purpose, but any with very rough or peeling bark will not do. Placement of the pattern where the stick will be held may also be desirable in some instances.

The process of bark carving begins with a pattern. It should be laid out first on paper (**Photo 63**). Doing this requires drawing a rectangle with one dimension equal to the height of the pattern desired and the other equal to the circumference of the staff where the design will be carved. The pattern can then be developed in outline form within the rectangle. Several designs attained by sketching different arrangements are recommended for making a selection.

The next step in the process involves drawing the pattern on the staff. This can be done freehand, with a few measured spots marked on the staff to guide the outlining. A felt-tip pen

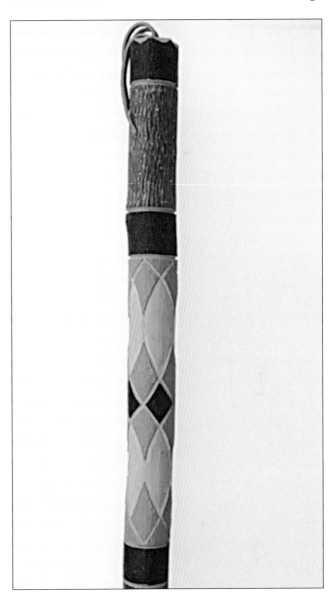

Photo 62:   Attractive geometric patterns can be carved and painted on bark-covered sticks.

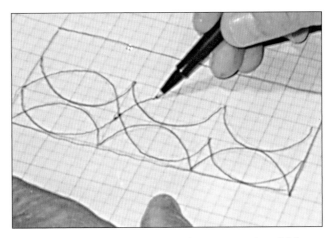

Photo 63:   A pattern for bark carving should be laid out on paper to establish size and detail.

Photo 64:   Carving proceeds by incising along outlines and then removing sections within.

seems to mark the bark as effectively as anything. The outlines thus drawn serve to guide the carving knife for incising around sections and removing the parts desired **(Photo 64)**. Notice that a pattern can be given a different appearance by alternating the sections of bark removed. Thus, in the stick shown the sections removed to reveal the inner wood could be left standing and some of the painted bark removed instead. The difference in appearance can be amazing.

Carving spiral forms

As with many bark-carved designs, spiral patterns are geometric **(Photo 65)**. The helical shapes are created by incising. Completed

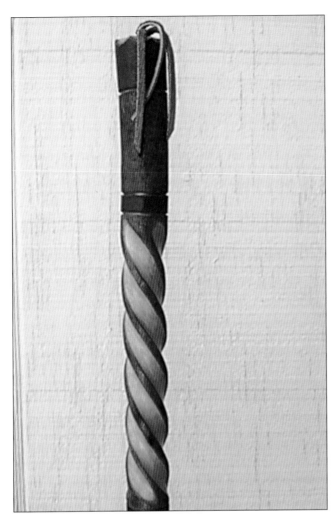

Photo 65: A spiral design, a helix, is usually several spirals combined in a decoration.

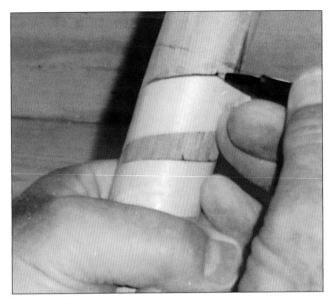

Photo 66: The use of tape to guide the felt-tip pen will help assure uniformity in the layout.

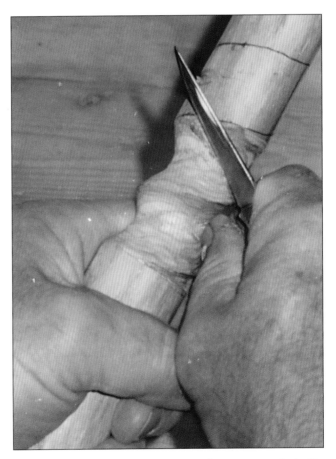

Photo 67: Spirals can be carved on a round staff, surprisingly perhaps, with relative ease.

patterns may be, and often are, several spirals intertwined.

The carving of a spiral follows the layout of a guideline. Whether to place the carving above or at the spot where the stick will normally be grasped can be decided by how much the carving is needed for gripping. Whatever the case, masking tape entwined about the staff assists in obtaining a uniform spiral. This process is shown in **Photo 66**. Be aware that the tightness of spiral results directly from the lead stepped along the stick when wrapping the tape. The lead, the spiral's spacing, definitely determines the carving's appearance, but it does not appreciably affect incising **(Photo 67)**.

Photo 68: Naturalistic representations of animals are commonly used to top walking sticks.

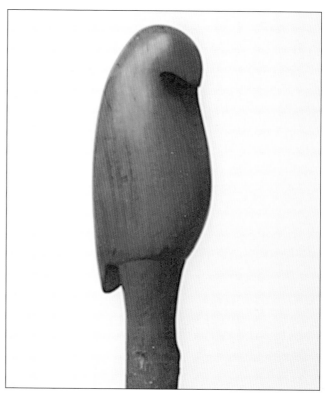

Photo 69: Designers often prefer stylizing because of the artistic interpretation involved.

Photo 70: Carvings in the round originate by drawing front and side views to guide the saw.

Figures for men and boys

Although the geometric patterns described in the proceeding sections offer a desirable change, many people prefer the three-dimensional carving of naturalistic figures as a way of decorating walking sticks. Carvings of animals are widely accepted for that purpose. Walking sticks topped with the kinds of figures which men, and some boys, would likely be most happy to receive are illustrated in this section.

Photo 68 shows a realistic carving in the round attached to the upper end of a staff. The use of a reddish-brown stain on the basswood owl helps duplicate its red phase and blend with the staff's bark. A firm joint and strong glue hold the figure securely in place.

By way of contrast, a stylized owl in cherry wood is shown in **Photo 69**. The carving has only the general shape of an owl, but what it represents leaves no doubt. The artistic interpretation involved in stylizing a figure like this will sometimes be preferred to a strict duplication of nature. All carvings in the round, whether

Photo 71:   A cobra on a walking stick is likely to be preferred mostly by men and boys.

Photo 72:   The cobra has been carved in basswood, lightly stained, and sparingly painted.

stylized or naturalistic, ordinarily begin with a sketch of the figure's front and side views on a block of wood.

A roughed-out form (**Photo 70**) is then removed for carving by band sawing along the outlines. Blocks of wood, each 2-5/8 inches square by 5-1/2 inches long, will accommodate carvings of the owls illustrated above.

Photographs of other figures known to evoke the interest of men and boys are presented here. **Photos 71** and **72** show a cobra in two views

Photo 73:   Observers of this mythical creature just seem unable to resist talking about it.

made naturalistic in appearance by staining and painting selected portions. The maximum dimensions of this attachment, in inches, are 3-1/4 x 3-1/4 x 8 inches. Most girls and women are not likely to want to carry a stick decorated with such a figure.

Probably, too, a staff with a mythical dragon on top would be welcome only by a few females as a companion on a stroll through the park. **Photo 73** shows one made 3-1/2 inches wide, 5 inches deep, and 8 inches high. Like the cobra, the dragon's head is carved from basswood, carefully attached to a staff, and colored appropriately. While affection for the stick with the mythical creature secured on top has often been outspoken, it is to be recognized that a figure carved as shown can be easily damaged. Its handling generally requires special care, but taking the ornately carved figure into brush-covered areas is not recommended at all.

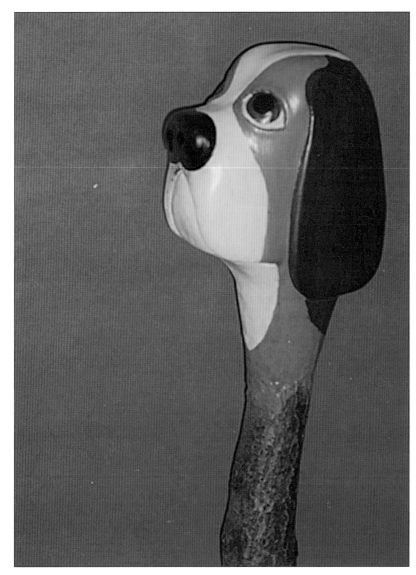

Photo 74:   A hound dog might be the kind of companion enjoyed most on a walking stick.

The painted hound, **Photo 74**, carries little of that concern. It has none of the sharp, delicate projections needing special attention and protection. As carved, the piece's overall measurements are 2-1/2 inches by 5 inches by 5 inches. The design is one more example of how to effectively style a three-dimensional decoration. Is the facial expression true to life?

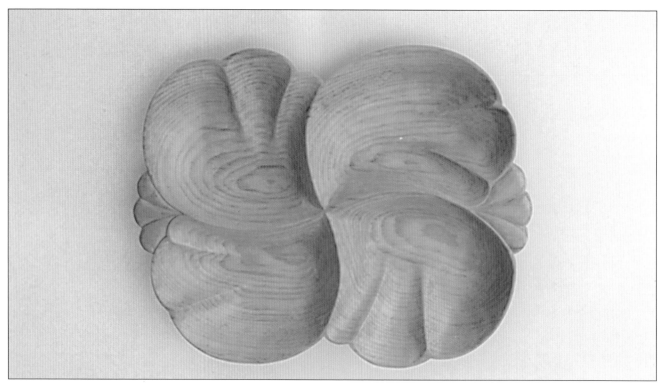

Photo 75: A tray can be artistic yet effective for holding several varieties of snacks at once.

5. Honor Thy Parents

Parents and grandparents deserve special recognition, so our federal government has decreed. Mothers, fathers, and grandparents now have days set aside during the year for the purpose of directing attention to them and their personal achievements. Close relatives customarily honor elders with greeting cards and gifts on or near the dates designated.

National holidays for recognizing certain people of advanced years came into being in this country during the twentieth century. Mother's Day came first, being proclaimed by President Wilson in 1914 an event for observance annually. The second Sunday in May was designated the official time for the event. Father's Day became a national holiday to be observed on the third

Photo 76:   The carving about this vessel serves to enhance an otherwise plain appearance.

Sunday in June when President Nixon signed it into law in 1972, and Grandparent's Day followed suit when, in 1978, President Carter officially set aside the first Sunday after Labor Day for its observance. The reason given for observing Grandparent's Day in the fall was unique. Grandparents, as occurs with the leaves of vegetation during that season, were noted also for showing signs of decline.

What kind of a gift might be given to those honorees? In that they are likely to have established residences, something for the home could be fitting. A skillfully handcrafted piece is recommended. Whether it has a practical purpose or is strictly decorative may depend on individual circumstances.

Make it practical

To be practical, an article must serve some useful purpose. Bowls and trays generally fit this category. Some are splendidly artistic, as well. Not only do many serve the useful purpose of holding and conveying fruit, nuts, and other snack foods of various kinds, some also display a beauty of form besides that inherent in the wood's grain. Form and function have an integral relationship in the making of bowls and trays. A dull or monotonous shape resulting from devoting attention primarily to the

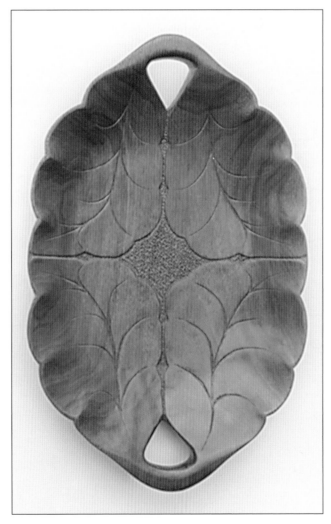

Photo 77:   The shallow carving in the center also influenced the tray's shape along its sides.

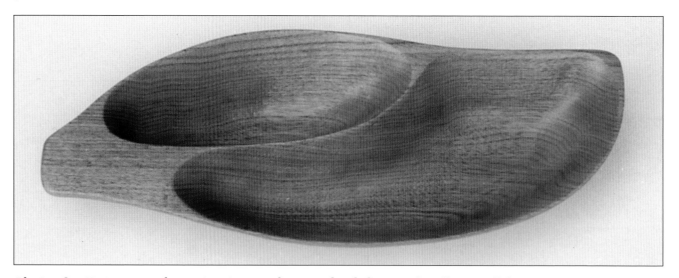

Photo 78:   Nature may be an inspirational source for defining a bowl's overall form.

practical requirements may sometimes be enhanced by adding decorative carvings in appropriate spots. The best combinations may, indeed, make highly prized gifts.

Consider the uniquely designed four-compartment tray shown in **Photo 75**, previous page. Its dimensions are 1-3/8 x 9-1/2 x 12-1/4 inches. The wood is pine. The finish is clear, satin, and non-toxic. Any beauty to be ascribed to the tray derives from the craftsman's effort to create an artistic form that functions as intended. That the piece will effectively hold several snacks at once for passing among guests or family seems evident. Its artistic quality may, on the other hand, be judged variously by individual viewers.

Additional ideas for designing bowls and trays are presented below to assist in selecting a gift. An example containing a decoratively carved perimeter, the purpose of which is simply to avoid the starkness of a plain border, is shown in **Photo 76**. It is made of cherry wood to the overall dimensions 1-9/16 inches by 7-3/4 inches by 14-3/8 inches. **Photo 77** is a reproduction of a walnut tray, 1-5/8 inches by 8 inches by 12-1/4 inches, in which a centrally carved relief decoration has also influenced the form around the perimeter. In still another example, **Photo 78** shows a butternut bowl with a shape inspired by a leaf growing in nature. Its size is 1-3/4 inches by 4-1/2 inches by 11 inches. The thickness

Photo 79: A work-holding jig of some kind serves an essential purpose when gouging bowls and trays.

of the wood in each of these items is such that weight does not seem excessive or burdensome.

The procedure for making a tray or bowl is essentially the same for all. The process begins by creating or borrowing a design and selecting wood of appropriate species and size. Next, an outline of the article is drawn on the wood. The piece is then sawed along the outline on a band saw and later carved internally with handheld gouges and mallet. The carving, **Photo 79**, can best be done using a wooden jig. A guide for gouging the vessel's cavities to the depth desired and not beyond can be created by first drilling several holes with a Forstner bit to the depth intended for the carving. Wall thicknesses of about 5/16 of an inch are generally adequate. Final smoothing after gouging and abrading should be done with a goose-neck scraper **(Photo 80)**.

Decorative relief carving and stippling, the latter shown being done in **Photo 81**, follows most other steps in construction. Notice that a short piece of dowel rod surrounds the nail for ease in holding when stippling. Also, notice that the wood around the article's perimeter remains at full thickness, thereby, providing a solid backing until all shaping operations are complete. The edges are finally undercut on a band saw and

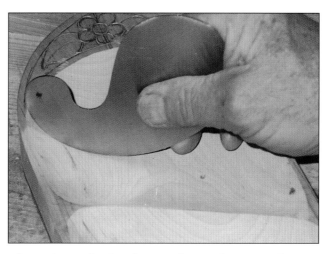

Photo 80: The final smoothing of a gouged cavity is done with a goose-neck scraper.

Photo 81: A decorative carving on a bowl is preferably made shallow and stippled.

Photo 82:   This view shows the undercutting generally required along a vessel's perimeter.

Photo 83:   A decoration showing patriotism for one's country is a desirable gift for many.

sanded smooth before applying a sealer. An angled view of the finished cherry bowl, **Photo 82,** shows the result of undercutting about the perimeter. Its measurements are 1-1/2 x 5-3/4 x 12-1/2, in inches.

Decorative choices

An ornament for hanging on a wall might also be considered for giving, whether to a parent or to grandparents. To be suitable there must be a place where the decoration can be displayed properly, and its motif must be appropriate for the recipient. Symbolic pieces, particularly, must be analyzed for their appropriateness.

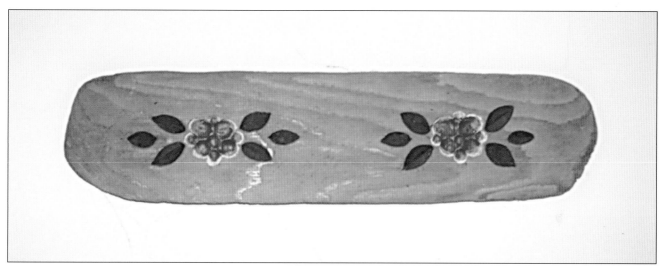

Photo 84: A decorated piece of driftwood might be fittingly displayed in a fisherman's den.

A display of patriotic design is shown in **Photo 83**. Its dimensions overall are 2 inches deep, 9-1/2 inches high, and 22 inches wide. The carved eagle is lightly stained butternut, with thin coats of white and yellow acrylic paints covering certain features to add a touch of realism. Black paint dots the eye. Black paint also covers the lettering incised in the poplar-wood ribbon in order to make the motto stand out. This piece represents the kind of gift that both men and women would probably appreciate receiving.

Another piece in this category, a comparatively simple example, is the plaque pictured in **Photo 84**. This rustic creation might be hung in a den. It is a piece of driftwood that has been decorated with incised, painted, floral carvings. Its dimensions are 3/8 inch by 3 inches by 12-1/2 inches. Anyone desiring to make a rustic decoration similar to this one might consider using weathered wood. Such wood might be more easily acquired than driftwood.

Photo 85 shows a piece of different design made for hanging in a home or office. This one features a floral carving in bold relief. The design has realistic qualities, although no effort was made to duplicate nature exactly. The wood is pine, with dimensions 1-1/8 inches by 5-3/8 inches by 18-1/4 inches. The only finish applied is satin polyurethane. An interesting feature of this plaque is that the pine will turn deeply orange with age.

Photo 85:   Wall decorations carved in bold relief may serve beautifully in a home or office.

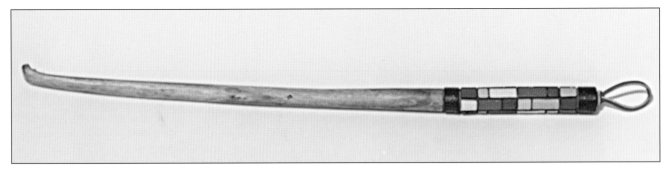

Photo 86   A colorful device like this must also have the tip shaped properly for scratching.

Photo 87:   Incise rectangular outlines to carve the backscratcher's handle.

An article made of wood should be hung in a special way. The recommended way is to first drill or carve an upwardly slanted slot into its backside. The hole must be above and in line with the article's center of gravity. This method enables the decoration to remain straight and flush against the wall when hung on a projecting nail head. Although a wooden article could be hung by attaching a manufactured hanger to its backside, the projecting bulk would not let the article rest flat against the wall.

More useful gifts

When deciding what parents and grandparents can use, consider one of these small, useful, wooden articles: a back scratcher, a sharp instrument for opening letters or a container for holding toothpicks conveniently by the dinner table. All are appropriate for elders, and the wood may cost little. Much of it, if bark-covered, could cost no more than the time needed for gathering and carving the pieces. A possible supply of the wood may be nearby. The small trees and branches that tree trimmers treat as

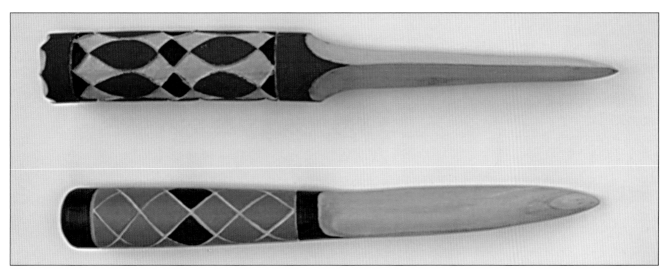

Photo 88:   These colorful letter openers are positioned to show the blades from two angles.

waste might be a source for obtaining wood without charge, and that growing in a neighbor's yard or wood lot just might be another free source.

A branch of a tree can be readily made into a backscratcher (**Photo 86**). A slightly curved piece no more than an inch in diameter and 20 inches long will suffice. The bark must be relatively smooth and tightly attached. If the wood is green, a section should be cut several inches longer on each end than the finished piece is to be. Doing that will allow for removing the ends that may check while drying. When cut to length, the bark should be shaved away except for about six inches where the handle will be. The bare length can then be tapered to a hooked point using a spokeshave. This step may be followed by carving and painting the bark on the handle.

All sorts of designs are possible, but the one shown being carved for this application in **Photo 87** is an irregular sequence of rectangles that later will be painted in brilliant colors. A coat of satin polyurethane overall will protect the piece from excessive wear and erosion of the colors during use. A loop of leather projecting from the handle is useful for hanging the scratcher on a hook.

To make a letter opener, cut a 9-inch section from dry sapling or branch of approximately 1 inch thickness (**Photo 88**). Use a hard wood that will maintain the sharpness necessary for

Photo 89: Bark-covered poplar wood can be made into a useful piece for the diner table.

Photo 91: Nature's inspiration, as in a floral relief carving, may be the preferred adornment.

Photo 90: Basswood toothpick holders also make desirable items when chip carved.

opening letters. The piece may be stripped of all bark, although smooth and firmly attached bark may be left for carving the hand grip. About half of a piece's length is then tapered to the tip to form a thin, wide blade with sharp cutting edges. A spokeshave accomplishes this readily. As explained in the previous chapter, the procedure for a applying a design to a round, bark-covered handle entails drawing a pattern full size on paper, transferring the pattern to the wood, carving the pattern so that sections stand in relief, painting the pattern with acrylic colors, and applying a clear finish overall. Bear in mind that geometric patterns can be produced on handles whether or not covered with bark. Only the manner of carving will be slightly different.

Toothpick holders are other useful gifts that can be made from dry wood covered with smooth, tight bark (**Photo 89**). Branches or saplings about 1-1/2 inches in diameter will suffice when cut to a length of 2-1/4 inches. The pieces must be bored on center for holding the toothpicks. A hole 1 inch in diameter and 1-5/8 inches deep is recommended. For decoration, the bark may be incised and painted in patterns of choice.

Toothpick holders made from blocks of basswood measuring 1-3/4 wide by 1-1/2 inches deep by 2-7/8 inches high are shown in **Photo 90** and **Photo 91**. These, also, are bored on center, preferably with a Forstner bit. They make attractive table pieces when the broader surfaces are chip carved or carved in relief.

Out of the past

An unusual, perhaps humorous, article for the home harks back to the days when figures representing Uncle Sam were often used to support mail boxes in rural areas of the United States. The article shown here, **Photo 92**, is made from an old fence post, which could be another reason why some people will express interest in having one. An Uncle Sam like this could be used for decoration alone, or it could be used also for holding letters prepared for mailing.

Uncle Sam's body can be made from a post or straight branch of about 4 inches diameter, the feet from a 1-1/2 inch board, the arms and hat rim from 3/4 inch boards, and the horizontal letter support from thin Masonite. While the figure's height is 31 inches, that dimension could be increased or decreased to suit. In any case, only a small amount of carving is needed. The use of patriotic colors does much to produce the effect wanted.

Photo 92:   How old would a parent or grandparent have to be to enjoy this letter holder?

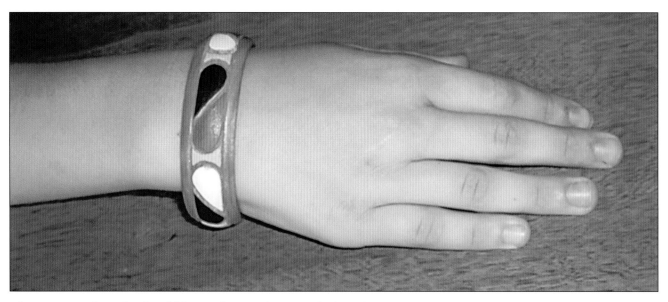

Photo 93:   A bangle should be no larger than needed to slip over the wearer's folded hand.

6.   Don't Overlook Graduation

Graduation is an important event for a family. It signifies that one of the members has now successfully completed the requirements for moving onto a new pursuit. Whether having just completed high school or college studies, a graduating student ordinarily receives the praise of all concerned along with a gift from parents. The gift, besides signifying parental appreciation and admiration, may also serve as a reminder of past associations and an inspiration to strive for a rewarding future.

As in gift-giving generally, the more known about a graduate's interests and needs the easier will be the decision about what to give. Will it be something of use now or more useful in the future? What lifestyle does the graduate have, and what goals does he or she hope to accomplish? Answers to these and similar questions will help define what kind of gift seems most suitable.

Girl's stuff
Jewelry seems to be a favorite of females of all ages, and there are numerous varieties and styles to choose from. In addition to those presented earlier, the bangles and barrettes presented in this section are also worthy of consideration when selecting awards for graduates. Bangles are usually worn on the wrist for their decorative effect. Barrettes are clips made for the useful purpose of clasping a girl's or woman's hair together in the back or to the side of the head. Any of these varieties shown could provide the personal effect desired.

Wooden bangles are shaped in circular form for the strength rings provide. They must be sized for slipping over the wearer's folded hand yet not be so large as to slip off or feel uncomfortably loose. An inside diameter of 2-3/8 inches seems to be about average, but some individuals may require larger or smaller sizes.

Photo 94:   The variety of designs possible is further indicated by these patterns.

As to style, there are many options. One is a painted abstraction, such as the bracelet being worn in **Photo 93**. It is decorated by outline incising and coloring with acrylic paints. The material is cherry wood finished to a width of 3/4 inch, 2-3/8 inches diameter inside, and 2-7/8 inches diameter outside. Its colorful appearance seems likely to have widespread appeal.

Two other styles are shown in **Photo 94**. The floral design decorates a cherry-wood bangle, the size of which is similar to the previous one except for its 7/8 inch width. The larger bangle with a chip-carved decoration about its circumference is made of catalpa wood. Both items are finished without the application of paint or stain.

To make a bangle, several factors must be kept in mind besides size. For reasons of strength and ease in carving, have the concentric circles formed by the bangle follow closely the annual rings of the wood by drawing on the end grain of cured stock. An illustration of this practice is shown in **Photo 37** on page 30. Next, saw off a section slightly larger in thickness than the bangle's width. The piece can then be sawed outside and inside to the diameters desired. This step may be followed by sanding on a drum sander, as illustrated for a walnut bangle in **Photo 95**. The carving may then proceed if, as shown in **Photo 96**, the wood has the strength of

Photo 95:   A drum sander in a drill press is especially useful for smoothing a bangle inside.

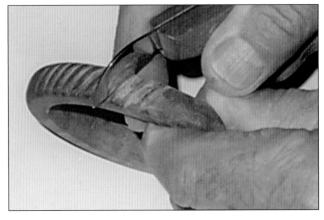

Photo 96:   A strong wood, such as walnut, may be carved after removing the central wood.

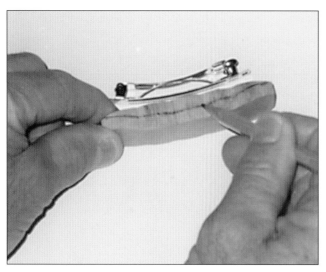

Photo 97: The curvature of a barrette's clasp must be precisely duplicated on the ornament.

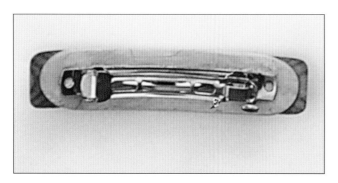

Photo 99: A hair clasp is centered backside when attaching it to the decorative piece.

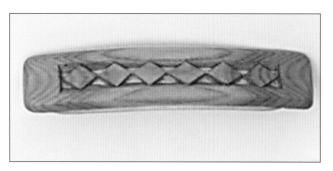

Photo 100 The carving on a lamination is most interesting when both woods are revealed.

Photo 98: The repetitively incised design is an important component of this barrette.

walnut or other hard wood. A softer, weaker wood may best be carved outside with the center section still in place.

Wooden barrettes must also be prepared in a particular way. Metal clasps used to back-up the decorative attachments are curved, necessitating that the decorations be curved similarly for gluing in place. In addition, the attachments must be longer and wider than the metal clasps in order to hide them when set in the hair. **Photo 97** is a side view of a piece of cherry wood being prepared for sawing on the precise arc necessary for gluing to a clasp. Its width of 3/4 inch and length of 3-1/2 inches will adequately cover the slightly smaller metal clasp.

The finished barrette is shown being worn in **Photo 98**. The carved decoration, the wood used, and the size of the piece are among the options possible. Metal clasps, too, are sometimes available in several lengths.

Further variations in design may be obtained by laminating woods before carving and assembling then onto a clasp. A barrette of papaw wood laminated over a shorter and wider piece of basswood is shown in a back view, **Photo 99**, and a front view, **Photo 100**. Although the finished lamination is only 1/4 inch thick, close inspection reveals that the carving went through the papaw but not through the basswood. Of utmost concern is the exactness of curvature needed for laminating the pieces.

For the boys

Depending on what the graduating student plans to do, he might prepare for certain future situations which were not likely to have been experienced during his time in school. He may, as often occurs in life after education, encounter situations where dress in formal attire becomes practically essential. A necktie neatly tied and clasped to the shirt could be particularly important for someone applying for a job in the business world or when calling on a client. Then, too, meetings occur where everyone in attendance is expected to wear a nametag. A person wearing a carved nametag, rather than the usual paper variety, will likely place the wearer a notch apart and in that way help to function as an ice-breaker in the crowd.

A handcrafted tie clasp is shown in place in **Photo 101**. It is small, being only 3/8 inch thick by 1/2 inch wide by 2 inches long. The decoration is a simple line carving which conforms effectively to the shape given the wood. A side view, **Photo 102**, reveals the type of clasp used to complete the assembly. A tie tack, shown in **Photo 103** beside the clasp, uses a toggle and pin for attaching the tie to a shirt. The wood in both the clasp and the tack is cherry.

Nametags have more-than-usual permanence when made of wood, but they must not be too bulky. They must feel comfortable when pinned

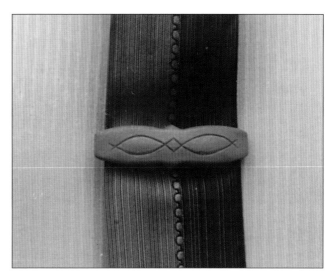

Photo 101: A graduate might profit by wearing a tie clasp where traditional dress is expected.

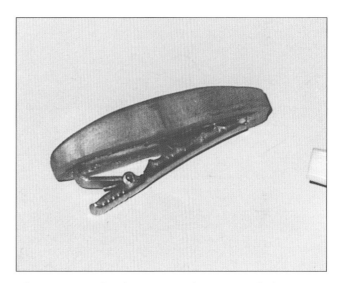

Photo 102: The decorative cherry wood shown here is glued to a slightly altered metal clasp.

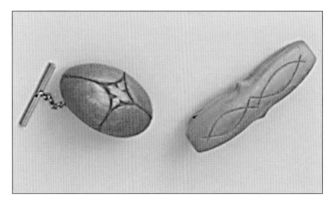

Photo 103: Careful incising can effectively enhance a form, as the tie clasp and tie tack show.

Photo 104:   A section of a tree limb with smooth bark attached makes a unique nametag.

Photo 105:   Carving through the outer bark reveals the harmonious color of the inner bark.

Photo 106:   This identifier will surely elicit attention in a meeting where nametags are worn.

to one's shirt or coat. It is equally important to create a suitable style. A rustic nametag, for example, would seem to be appropriately worn in gatherings or situations where people are less formally attired.

A photograph of a bark-covered nametag may be seen in **Photo 104**. The piece is 1/2 inch thick in the middle by 2 inches wide by 2-3/4 inches long. The outer and inner bark have a combined thickness of 1/16 of an inch, with the outer bark being darker than the inner bark and much darker than the wood underneath. Some differences appear in the incised lettering, **Photo 105**. The only paint applied is a thin wash of white along the deeply incised perimeters of the letters – a technique for making the name stand out vividly.

A more elaborately carved nametag is illustrated in **Photo 106**. The faces of the letters in relief are painted silver, a final step before spraying with a sealing coat. A rope-like carving decorates the article, the dimensions of which, in inches, are 5/16 by 1-5/8 by 4. Again, the wood used is cherry.

His or hers

Want to give a gift that both boys and girls would enjoy? How about a carved fraternity pin or school logo for one to wear, or maybe something to hold pencils and pens for use by the high school graduate who will be moving into a dormitory room? The several examples presented here are indicative of what can be done, but the woodcarver might consider decorating those gifts with the logo or name of the school or college specifically involved. A design incorporating that feature could be most appealing.

The construction of a fraternity pin follows the procedure previously described for making hat and lapel pins. With a design in mind, the pin's outline is drawn on a piece of tupelo or basswood **(Photo 107)**. Wood about 5/16 of an inch thick will suffice. That thickness will adequately support relief carving on a piece 1 inch wide by 1-1/2 inches long. After sawing and

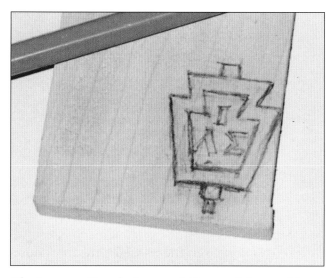

Photo 107:   Tupelo is especially good for making a wearable fraternity pin or school logo.

Photo 108:   A gold background and Greek letters in black aid in the fraternity's identification.

carving the pin to the shape desired, a bit of color should be added so that the fraternity's Greek letters stand out. As usual, the piece should be finished with a clear sealer. A pin-and-clutch finding attached to the pin's back prepares it for wearing.

A finished pin may be given a visible position on one's clothing, as shown in **Photo 108**. While this example displays the keystone form used by a particular academic fraternity, it shows that a bit of careful carving and painting can contribute to legibility. Being noticeable and readable is, after all, an important reason for wearing such a pin.

While a fraternity or school pin is made primarily for show, a pen and pencil holder has a practical application as its primary purpose. A carved decoration might be added to such a container to increase its desirability. **Photo 109** shows a holder made of catalpa wood that has been incised with a simple, but colorful design. The article has an outside diameter mid-center of 2-3/4 inches and a height of 4-3/8 inches. The inside bore is 2-3/8 inches in diameter by 3-5/8 inches deep. Its usefulness seems apparent.

Photo 109:   A useful gift for the desk could be exactly what a college student needs.

Photo 110: An expertly carved scene is certain to be admired when displayed in a student's dormitory room. Carving by Tom Meyer.

Photo 111: This sculpture is most likely to interest those who see beauty in abstract form.

Dorm room adornments

For the graduate preparing to move into a room in a college's residence hall, a decorative item of some kind may be the conversation piece he or she will find helpful for making friends. A three-dimensional carving made for displaying on a desk or shelf could fit the situation. Depending on one's interests, it could be naturalistic or abstract in design.

An expertly carved assembly is shown in **Photo 110**. The life-like details given the bear and hornet's nest effectively complement the section of branch representing the tree trunk. It is a well-made piece that does not take up much space. It is 9 inches tall. The dimensions of the oval base are 4 inches by 5 inches, and the carved bear has an extended length of 5 inches. The quality of the piece would surely invite the admiration of anyone who enjoys carvings in natural form.

For the person interested in form other than an exact duplication of nature, a sculpture having an abstract quality may be preferred. The accompanying photograph, **Photo 111**, displays one such sculpture. The wood is butternut. It is 2-1/2 inches deep at the base, 4 inches wide, and 16-3/8 inches high. Any beauty attributable to the piece likely derives from the wood's natural grain and the form created by carving. While not originally intended to represent existing form, the piece is now titled. This is a consequence of knowing how viewers often try to determine what an untitled sculpture represents. Thus, it has meaning becoming to representational abstractions. Apply the title "Where There's Smoke." Doesn't that play on words now suggest something specific about the swirling spirals reaching skyward? Perhaps, college students viewing the sculpture would enjoy creating other titles.

Photo 112:   These brooches are intended for the secretary who likes nonrepresentational art.

7. Remember Secretary's Day

Do you work closely with a secretary? Maybe you're related to one. Either way, you can make that person's day enjoyable with a gift.

Secretary's Day is celebrated during Secretaries Week, which occurs during the third week in April. Origin of the celebration is being debated today. Some contend it grew out of efforts by card companies to create another day for giving gifts, and others point to evidence it actually resulted from substantial efforts in 1952 to acknowledge and appreciate the hard work of those office assistants. In any case, the celebration continues. Unlike other occupation-based holidays, Secretary's Day comes with the expectation of giving a gift to a worthy recipient.

Assuming the one you expect to honor is female, any gift along the lines previously suggested for women could be suitable. An item covered in this chapter might be better yet.

Jewelry to wear, something for her desk, or an article for her home are the basic categories recommended.

Something she is known to favor is most highly recommended for giving. Find out beforehand what style she likes. Engage her in casual conversation. She'll tell you what you need to know. Both the kind of article and how she prefers it to be decorated can be determined in that way.

Secretaries usually like jewelry. Items of personal adornment are especially apt for the one who must always look her best for a boss or before the public. An individually crafted bracelet, brooch, or coordinated set that cannot be obtained commercially could send a message about one's regard for her. The carved items which follow have that one-of-a-kind quality. The problem is to determine which article and which style will be most appealing.

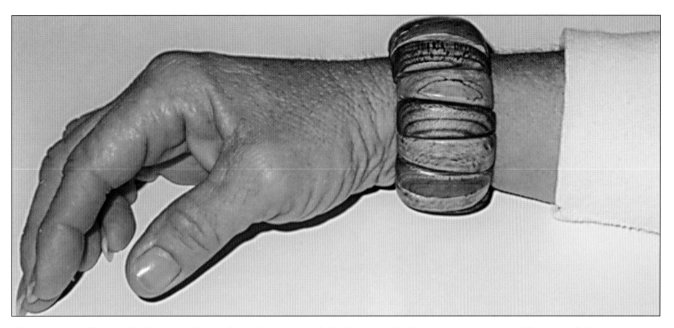

Photo 113:   Size and choice of wood are important factors in designing an expansible bracelet.

Nonrepresentational forms

Photo 112 shows a pair of brooches made for pinning to a jacket or blouse. Neither represents anything in existence. As such, they are abstractions. Any beauty one beholds in pieces of this style relates to the wood's grain, color, and finished form. The single-piece brooch illustrated is made from walnut, 3/8 inch by 1-3/8 inches by 2-7/16 inches. The multi-piece brooch is comprised of curved pieces of papaw, tupelo, and cherry wood. Its overall size is 1/2 inch by 2-1/8 inches by 2-1/2 inches, with the thickness of the individual pieces varying from 1/16 inch to 1/4 inch. A curved blade, is used for carving the curvatures in a brooch of this style.

Another nonrepresentational piece, an expansible bracelet, is shown being worn in **Photo 113**. It combines compatible woods, papaw and ackee. Nine individual pieces of each wood are arranged alternately and held together with two hidden strands of elastic cord designed for that purpose. The assembly's inside diameter is 2 inches, its outside diameter is 3 inches, and its width is 1-7/16 inches. The most critical dimension is the inside circumference around the wearer's wrist. This measurement is important for obtaining a comfortable fit.

The construction of a bracelet of similar design

Photo 114:   Most secretaries would be proud to wear a brooch like this Dove of Peace.

Photo 115:   A special jig is needed for drilling the tapered pieces to receive the elastic cord.

necessitates the tapering of pieces end to end and outside to inside. Each piece in the example tapers 1/2 inch to 3/16 inch from one end to the other, and the inside of each piece at its thickest point is 1/16 inch less than its outside. A jig of special design simplifies drilling for the elastic cord **(Photo 115)**. In place of papaw, which is not generally available commercially, and ackee, a Jamaican wood rarely imported, other woods having beautiful grain or contrasting colors may be used with good results.

As holds true for most brooches, an expansible bracelet could be worn at the workplace. It would enhance one's attire without obtrusively interfering with secretarial duties. Loose or dangling jewelry, on the other hand, could be a problem.

Animal and floral forms

The Dove of Peace shown in **Photo 114** is a brooch that many would be proud to wear. The naturalistic style leaves no doubt about its representation. Carved from a piece of tupelo 3 inches square by 9/16 inch thick, the dove

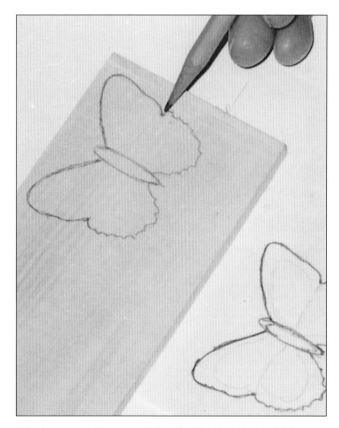

Photo 116: These brooches, one stylized and one naturalistic, are for those who like animals.

carries a simulated olive branch that has been made using wood chips for leaves, wire for the stem, glue to hold the pieces together, and acrylic paint to produce realistic color. The whiteness of the bird is natural.

Photo 116 illustrates two other brooches, one stylized and the other more realistic. What the figures represent seems obvious. Style of representation, rather than the creatures represented, would very likely dominate individual decisions about which brooch is preferred.

Both brooches are light in weight. The butterfly measures 1-3/4 inches by 2-1/2 inches at its largest points. Its outline is shown being drawn in **Photo 117** on a piece of tupelo 1/4 inch thick. This allows for giving the thinly carved wings sufficient dihedral. By way of contrast in style and construction, two woods are combined to form the cat. The figure has a basswood base, the dimensions of which are 3/16 inch by 1-1/2 inches by 2-5/8 inches. The walnut overlays are semi-spherical pieces 3/4 inch and 1-1/8 inches in diameter.

Women generally like flowers, and secretaries are probably no different. However, the manner of representation may influence individual choices. The carved brooches illustrated in **Photo 118** indicate the differences possible. The colored brooch is most naturalistic, but the acrylic paint completely hides the wood. The piece wears well, because the use of a single block of basswood 2-1/2 inches square and 3/8 inch thick resulted in this floral piece being light in weight.

Photo 117: The wood for the butterfly is thick enough for carving the wings on a dihedral.

Photo 118:   Flowers are practically ideal for carving and arranging for wearing as brooches.

Moreover, it has no weak portions that could easily be broken off.

The two brooches made of woods in natural color are also of the proper weight and substantial construction. The basswood flowers are 1/4 inch thick. They are backed by strong, beautiful oval and circular forms in walnut and cherry. These are only 1/8 of an inch thick. Unlike basswood which sometimes seems bland when not stained or painted, the natural color and grain of the two back-up woods adds a measure of unaltered beauty to the assembly. Those who prefer to see carved wood left uncolored would likely choose one of the end pieces, the final selection of which could depend on the color of the garment available on which to wear it.

Gifts for stepping out

A neatly carved set of coordinated jewelry has an elegance that seems more suitable for wearing at a party or formal gathering than in the workplace. Moreover, a set including an article that hangs loosely about the neck or wrist could get in the way when performing certain tasks during the day's work. In any case, similarly decorated items impart a dressed-up look when worn together in a set.

Photo 119:   A coordinated set of jewelry will add elegance to one's dress.

What secretary wouldn't be happy to receive a set carved like that shown in **Photo 119**? Both the necklace and brooch feature a design uniformly carved in tupelo. Precise drawing and carving are important when creating a set with a repetitive design such as this. Size, too, is important. The brooch and the necklace's carving are each 5/16 inch thick. They are 1-15/16 inches and 1-3/4 inches in diameter, respectively. The gold beads on the cord are available commercially, and so are the wooden spacers, but the lengths of the wooden spacers are progressively shortened by carving to improve appearance. The cord is attached to the carving in two places by gluing its ends into small holes drilled into the wood.

For a more complete set, a pair of earrings in

Photo 120:   A smooth, glossy cabochon in walnut glued to basswood stands out vividly.

Photo 121:   A paper weight can be made comical, as well as a useful, for a secretary's desk.

matching style may be carved in tupelo and worn with the necklace and brooch. The earrings should be light in weight, each being made only 3/16 inch thick by 1-1/8 inches in diameter. They may be provided either with clips for unpierced ears or with pins for attaching to earlobes that have been pierced.

For a simpler gift, make a cabochon in wood. **Photo 120** Carve walnut wood to a smooth, convex shape, 1/4 x 7/8 x 1-1/2 in inches. Saw a piece of tupelo of 1/4 inch thickness to form an oval 1-1/8 inches by 1-7/8 inches. Scallop its perimeter, and attach a chain with a clasp for a necklace. Glue the smaller overlay to the tupelo, sand the assembly finely, and finish it with a glossy polyurethane. Attach the chain with a finding made for that purpose.

Items for her desk

Not all gifts for a secretary are for her personal adornment. Other possibilities are desk caddies and paper weights, articles that she could use at her work station. Paper weights anchor loose papers, and desk caddies hold small accessories in a handy location.

Photo 122:   A desk caddy is useful for holding paper clips, rubber bands, letter stamps, etc.

Photo 123:   Colorful felt glued inside a caddy improves its appearance and utility.

A paper weight is a particularly good gift, because it offers a variety of possibilities in design. If the secretary has a sense of humor, she might enjoy having a little carved mutt on her desk. **Photo 121** shows one such creation in use. The dimensions at its largest points are 1-7/8 inches wide, 3-3/4 inches long, and 2-3/4 inches high. To bring the little fellow up to a weight of about one-half pound, a hole can be bored into the interior from the bottom and filled with a quantity of BB shot.

A small box can serve conveniently as a desk caddy. It can hold paper clips, rubber bands, postage stamps, labels, or other small items used by a secretary. It can also be a decorative addition to her workplace. A desk caddy that has been turned on a lathe and decorated with a simple chip-carved pattern is shown in **Photo 122**. Made of basswood, the caddy has an outside diameter of 4-1/4 inches, a height of 3-1/4 inches, and a wall thickness of 5/16 inch. Its inside depth of only 2-5/8 inches provides for ease in reaching to the bottom. The accompanying photographs, **Photo 123** and **Photo 124**, reveal the

Photo 124:   Shown here is a more ornately carved container that a secretary might use.

felt-lined interior of the caddy and that of a more ornately decorated version.

Would she prefer some other design, say, something naturalistic in style? In that case, adapt a design from another section of this book or create your own. The basic idea is here, and only a little imagination is needed to create one's own pattern. Creating can, indeed, be very rewarding.

For her home

Different from anything presented to this point is a picture constructed in wood. Unusual though it may be, the picture has a quality many people are likely to enjoy.

A scene made entirely from different pieces of wood is shown in **Photo 125**. The frame in its assembled form is much like a shadow box. Made from 3/4 inch poplar, it is 4 inches deep by 21-1/2 inches square. The gray sky and dark forest simulations are made from pieces of weathered barn siding 5/8 inch thick. The moon is cherry wood 1/4 inch thick by 9 inches in diameter. The only carving in the entire assembly is that done to form the gull, which has a depth of 2 inches and a wing span of 12 inches. A twig from a tree adds to the naturalism of the scene. Only the gull is painted, and, as usual, a thin spray of satin polyurethane covers the entire assembly.

Because this form of picture has such extraordinary qualities, there may be some reluctance to attempt to duplicate it. Actually, constructing such a piece is easy. The difficult part could be obtaining weathered wood. If none can be had, the craftsman might consider using milled lumber. The sky might be left smooth, and the wood for the forest could be striated with a veining tool before applying stain. The finished result could be truly outstanding.

Photo 125: A scene made of weathered wood and carved work may be highly valued as a gift.

Photo 126:   A chip-carved cross is a gift for hanging at Christmas or other religious occasions.

8. For Holidays and Special Occasions

Holidays are days set aside for rest, recreation, and special observance. Originally established for observing holy days, holidays for nonreligious purposes have also become popular. Days for commemorating distinguished persons and secular events significant to the public are now commonplace.

In the United States, each state may establish its days of observance whether or not of religious orientation, while congress and the president make that determination for federal employees and the District of Washington. The states generally follow the federal government's lead.

Of the many holidays observed throughout the states, several have become traditional days for gift-giving. Those previously discussed, such as Valentine's Day and Secretary's Day, are among them, and, of course, so is Christmas. Many of these events seem to be observed as much for giving or exchanging presents as they are for the original purposes.

Numerous occasions besides the traditional holidays noted are observed with gifts. Retirement, marriage, the birth of a child, a promotion at work, moving into a new home, and paying off the mortgage are some of those occasions. Several widely recognized days are also ideal for presenting gag gifts. The laughter a humorous carving might create on April Fool's Day or Ground Hog Day, for example, could be just the spark family and friends need. Other events, too, such as a bachelor's party or an office party, are often fitting for awarding gifts done in a style that will generate a bit of mirth.

Something for Christmas

A special present for the person who closely observes this holy day is shown in **Photo 126**. It is the kind of gift that can be displayed during the holiday season or year-round by hanging it from a fireplace mantel or other fixture in the home. The cross is chip-carved tupelo, 3/8 inch thick by 3-1/2 inches wide and 5 inches high. The pattern and incised carver's symbol are optional. The finishing procedures follow those previously discussed for various articles.

A one-of-a-kind angel made for showing on a shelf would also be suitable for those interested in religious symbolism. A photograph of one carved in basswood and covered with acrylic paint is presented in **Photo 127**. She has a nondescript cherry-wood face in order to be generally representative, a halo made from electrical wire, and a small rose of peace in her grasp.

The angel's body was carved from stock 4-1/2 inches square by 12 inches long, with its wings being carved separately from pieces 3/4 inch by 3 inches by 6-3/4 inches. The wings were shaped

Photo 127: An angel, here styled to represent angels generally, furthers the meaning of Christmas.

Photo 128:   A small snowman carved in the round makes a very desirable tree ornament.

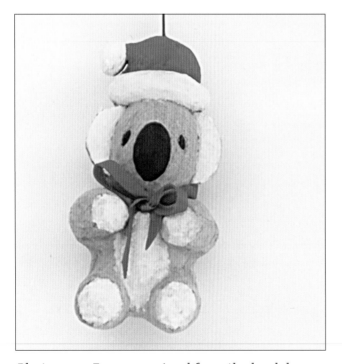

Photo 129:   Even an animal from the land down under can be fashioned to fit the season.

to about 3/8 of an inch thickness before gluing them in place. All parts of the completed figure were painted, except the face and rose.

Customarily, an evergreen tree is decorated in the home for the holiday season. Ornaments for giving as presents for that purpose or for displaying on one's own tree may be appropriate **(Photo 128)**. A little snowman carved from a piece of basswood about 2-5/8 inches in diameter and 4-1/2 inches long seems sure to be admired, especially if provided with a top hat, a means of inserting and holding a carved "candy" cane, and acrylic paint of suitable colors. A thin wire attached to the top will provide the necessary means of hanging.

Another ornament suitable for the tree can be carved in the form of a koala. This one might be most suitable as a present for someone especially familiar with the land down under. Give it seasonal attire, as shown in **Photo 129**, and it will garner a bit of deserved attention when hung on the tree.

Other items certain to be associated with Christmas, despite their secular orientation, are Little Rudy and Santa **(Photo 130)**. Notice that both articles are made from weathered wood. Santa is actually an old, checked fence post 3-1/2 inches in diameter cut to a length of 18-1/2 inches and carved. Cotton batting and acrylic paints are added for effect. Little Rudy is 8 inches long and stands 10 inches tall to the tip of its ears. The use of branch tips for antlers tops off the rustic figure. The presence of the pair during the holiday season would surely be enjoyed by youngsters.

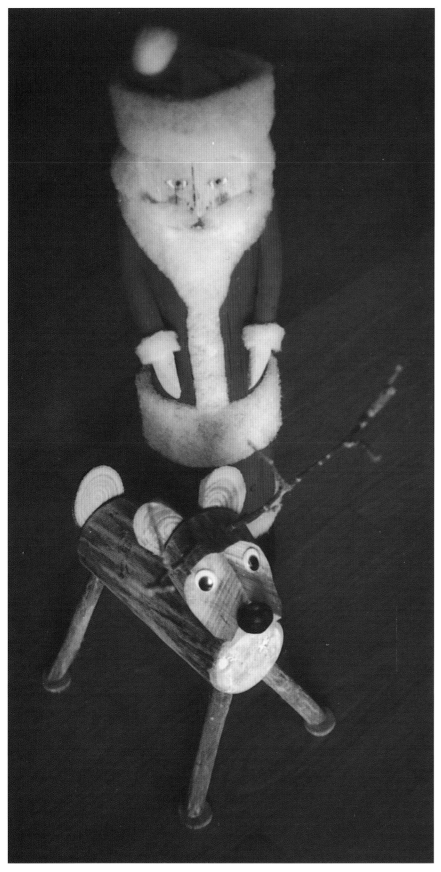

Photo 130:   Little Rudy and Santa, made of old posts and branches,
promote the holiday spirit.

IT'S MY GARDEN!

*Photo 131:
Here's a gift for gardeners, especially those who like cute little Easter bunnies.*

Something for other holidays

How about a little fun with someone who likes those cute little Easter bunnies? The assembly shown in **Photo 131** might just do, especially if that person has a garden which has been visited by the sharp-toothed critters. Carved from a piece of basswood 3-5/8 inches by 4 inches by 9 inches, the bunny is finished with a light stain and spot painted with acrylics. Of course, the cut-off plant and printed message do much to develop the humor.

Would you prefer to carve something similar but more to your originality? Consider this: a bunny dressed in a dinner jacket and with a message to the effect that "I know where the eatin's good," or "Keep those veggies coming." Take it from there. The possibilities are considerable. Let your creativity show as you develop an image and message of your own. It's fun.

Photo 132:   Once carved in wood, a pumpkin like this can be displayed year after year.

Photo 133:   A battery-activated light inside can also show off the horrible Halloween face.

A gift may be given on any holiday, even if customarily a time limited to exchanging cards only. That may be true for Thanksgiving. In any case, that day is one widely celebrated throughout the United States. A carved turkey would be an applicable gift.

Equally as fitting, perhaps, is the jack-o'-lantern on Halloween. Carve one in wood, then you will not have to do that again each year as you would if made from the real thing. What friend wouldn't want to receive such a present? Look at **Photo 132** and **Photo 133**. They are opposite views of a spherical carving in basswood, being only 5-1/2 inches in diameter. The article is the result of turning the shape inside and outside on a lathe, piercing the wood for the faces, carving external features, and applying paint to achieve the appearance of a real pumpkin. A 9-volt battery and a light that blinks when activated are inside. Such a creation adds a clever touch to a home's decor when displayed at the appropriate time of year.

For days widely recognized but observed mostly

Photo 134:   A facial expression can create a little mirth by relating it to a humorous incident.

Photo 135:   As shown on this walnut box, a design need not be elaborate to be effective.

for the fun of it, consider giving a humorous gift. A walking stick topped as shown in **Photo 134** could generate the reaction intended when given, for instance, on the first day of April. While having all the benefits and usefulness of the articles described in Chapter 4, a stick with a spherical ball can have a human expression painted on it to suit individual circumstances. It could be made to emulate any of a variety of human emotions, including one poking fun at a friend for committing a faux pas or some other surprising incident.

Useful gifts for all occasions

Wooden boxes made for setting on a dresser or other flat surface may be given as gifts for virtually any occasion. Women generally have jewelry and trinkets that must be stored when not in use. Indeed, some will use more than one container. In that a carved box will often be eagerly accepted, it may be thought of as a standby for awarding on whatever special occasion evolves.

Carved patterns, artistically applied, will provide a special effect. For best appearance, a carving should not be so elaborate or extensive as to dominate rather than enhance a box's appearance. A photograph of an example may be seen in **Photo 136**. Unlike carvings on articles made in some primitive cultures, where the patterns cover all visible surfaces, the catalpa box referred to here has a centrally carved floral

Photo 136: Boxes carved selectively let the wood's grain share the visual impact.

design with corner elements on its top only. Both the carved design and the beauty of the wood's grain stand out. The sunken relief carving is sufficiently decorative as applied.

The box is composed of wood planed to a thickness of 7/16 of an inch. It is 3-3/4 inches high, 5-1/2 inches wide, and 9-1/2 inches long. **Photo 137** shows the container with the lid open to reveal its felt-lined interior. Among other things, this piece shows what can be made from a billet once intended for burning in the fireplace.

A box of similar style, although of different material and decoration, is shown in **Photo 135**. Decorated with continuous carvings of holly leaves and berries, the container of walnut wood indicates how natural elements can be repeated to form a continuous, symmetrical design. The walnut wood has a firmness which holds carved detail well. As to manner of construction, the box is made much the same as others presented here. Its overall dimensions in inches, stated in the order of height, width, and length, are 5 by 6

Photo 137: A box will be most desirable for storing delicate ware if lined with colorful felt.

Photo 138:   A finish of clear, satin polyurethane adequately enhances and protects this box.

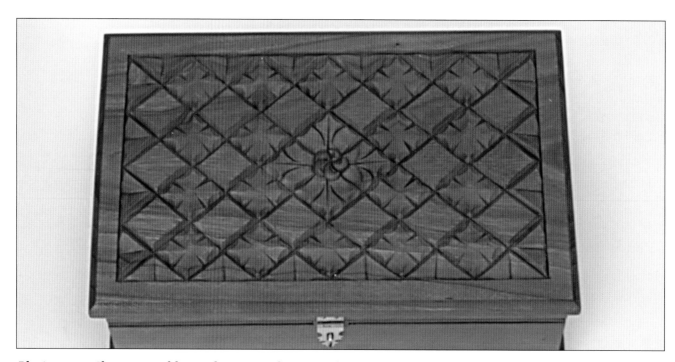

Photo 139:   Cherry wood has a firmness of texture that receives and holds carved detail well.

by 10-1/4. The wood's thickness is 1/2 inch.

Poplar wood also can be made into a beautiful box. Like tupelo and basswood, poplar has none of the grainy appearance resulting from contrasts due to summer and winter growth found in most woods. The chip-carved application illustrated in **Photo 138** seems to

bring the blandness of the homogeneous grain to life. It also shows a method of encompassing a circular element to make the pattern compatible with the lid's rectangular perimeter.

The box is 4 inches high, 6 inches wide, and 10 inches long. The wood's thickness is 1/2 inch. The finished piece, as has been done with other boxes in this section, is coated with a clear, satin polyurethane. As with the other boxes, the hardware may be fitted in place and then removed while applying the transparent finish.

Photo 139 shows a box that has a spectacular design carved all over its top surface. The wood is cherry, not a particularly easy material to carve but one that holds detail firmly. The dimensions of this box are 4 inches high, by 7 inches wide, by 11-1/4 inches long. The pieces are 7/16 of an inch thick, and the finished assembly is lined with felt of complementary color.

Decorative gifts for special events

Do you need a gift for someone about whom you know something special? Whatever the occasion, you might consider carving a present for a person that has meaning for that individual in some way. A decorative figure of some significance may be appreciated more than would a practical piece. For example, you might carve a bird in the round for someone known to be an avid bird-watcher. Or, how about giving a carved leprechaun to one who has visited Ireland? Associations of this order are considerable.

Photo 140:   A troll, Norway's mythological figure, is best given on certain special occasions.

The troll shown in **Photo 140** exemplifies this line of thinking. While the carving may be appropriately given for various reasons, it has a definite meaning for one who has relatives in Norway. Then, too, it would make a suitable piece for a person interested in collecting

Photo 141:   A realistic figure carved in the round could be the ideal gift for a naturalist.

mythical figures. Made for displaying on a shelf, the figure stands 9-1/2 inches tall, having been carved from a block of basswood 6 inches square by 10 inches long. Only the troll's walking stick with a dragon's head on the upper end has been carved separately.

For the individual who has an affinity for things in nature, a realistic figure carved in the round might be received more favorably than anything else. A squirrel, as shown in the accompanying photograph, **Photo 141**, is a possibility. The assembly has a height of 7-1/2 inches from the base of the stump to the top of the squirrel, and the squirrel is 6 inches in length from its nose to the tip of its tail. The natural materials used with the carved figure add an element or realism.

Do you still want more ideas? The carved gifts photographed and discussed throughout this text, including many previously suggested for holidays and events, are also applicable to many special occasions referred to here. Beyond that, use your imagination. The illustrations provide an excellent basis from which to proceed.

About the Author

James E. Seitz, Ph.D., formerly a college president and professor, devotes much of his time in retirement to woodcarving. He is an accomplished craftsman, having won ribbons for his entries in various shows and county-fair competitions for woodcarvers. He generally strives to carve pieces that are unique, pleasing to the eye, and practical in purpose. His products often attain a level of quality made possible by having studied design.

Jim is also an accomplished writer on the subject of woodcarving. In fact, this is the third of the ten books he has had published that are devoted specifically to the craft. One book, *Woodcarving: A Designer's Notebook*, applies many of the principles he studied in undergraduate school. Another, *Practical Woodcarving Design & Application*, emphasizes the means of bringing aesthetic and practical design together effectively, and a third book, though more generally applicable, is titled *Selling What You Make*. About a dozen of the many articles he has written pertain to woodcarving, as well.

Jim is an active participant and leader in civic affairs. He is uniquely honored by having been the founding president of six organizations, including a local senior center and an AARP chapter. He continues to hold positions of leadership as executive officer in an American Legion Post and mediator for the local Municipal Court. It, therefore, should come as no surprise that his credits also include having been a founder and the first president of a woodcarver's club in his home town. The club, founded in 1999, provides substantial support for his creative efforts.